Seneca: Th_   ___

DUCKWORTH COMPANIONS
TO GREEK AND ROMAN TRAGEDY

Series editor: Thomas Harrison

Also available

Euripides: Hippolytus
Sophie Mills

Euripides: Medea
William Allan

Seneca: Phaedra
Roland Mayer

Sophocles: Ajax
Jon Hesk

DUCKWORTH COMPANIONS
TO GREEK AND ROMAN TRAGEDY

Seneca: Thyestes

P.J. Davis

Duckworth

First published in 2003 by
Gerald Duckworth & Co. Ltd.
90-93 Cowcross Street, London EC1M 6BF
Tel: 020 7490 7300
Fax: 020 7490 0080
inquiries@duckworth-publishers.co.uk
www.ducknet.co.uk

A catalogue record for this book is available
from the British Library

ISBN 0 7156 3222 1

Printed and bound in Great Britain by
Biddles Ltd, *www.biddles.co.uk*

Contents

Acknowledgements

I would like to thank the following people who have helped me by their criticism, advice or specialist knowledge: Michael Bennett (University of Tasmania), Anthony Boyle (University of Southern California), Joost Daalder (Flinders University), Rhiannon Evans (University of Melbourne), Florence Dupont (Université Paris III), Michael Hurst, Jenna Mead (University of Tasmania), John Penwill (La Trobe University, Bendigo) and Marcus Wilson (University of Auckland).

I am also grateful to the Archive of Performances of Greek and Roman Drama at Oxford University for access to their files on *Thyestes* and for their hospitality, especially to Edith Hall, Pantelis Michelakis and Oliver Taplin. I owe a similar debt to Filippo Amoroso of the University of Palermo for his generous hospitality and for giving me a videotape of the production of *Thyestes* at Segesta in 1991.

Thanks are also due to Annette Fern, the Harvard Theatre Collection, Houghton Library, Harvard University and to the Billy Rose Theatre Collection at the Lincoln Center for the Performing Arts, New York, for responding so efficiently and helpfully to my inquiries.

I am happy to acknowledge the financial support of the Australian Research Council.

1

Contexts

Nero's Rome

At the time of Nero (who ruled AD 54-68) Rome was a city with a population of more than one million people controlling an empire which encircled the Mediterranean basin, an empire stretching from Syria to Britain, from the Danubian lands to North Africa.

Since 31 BC the Roman empire had been ruled by a single dynasty, the Julio-Claudians, established by Rome's first emperor, Augustus, who ruled from 31 BC to AD 14. Augustus had come to power through civil war and, in consequence, had attempted to conceal his power by preserving as far as possible the constitutional forms of the old republic. His successors, however, were less constrained by concern for legal appearances, and Nero, the last of the Julio-Claudians, inherited a well-established monarchy.

The historical tradition is relatively favourable towards the early years of Nero's reign, for it was the uninhibited cruelty and sexual depravity of his later years which made his name a byword for tyranny. But even the so-called *quinquennium Neronis*, the supposed five good years of Neronian rule,[1] was characterised by crime: power was seized on Nero's behalf through the assassination of Claudius, his adoptive father, in 54, and sustained by the murders of Britannicus, his brother by adoption, in 55, and Agrippina, his mother, in 59. There was also his leadership of a band of thugs in the streets, brothels and taverns of Rome, an activity which Tacitus dates to 56.[2]

Tacitus sees 62 as a significant turning-point,[3] for this was the year in which treason trials were restored, in which Burrus died and Seneca's power began to decline, in which Nero divorced and murdered his wife, Octavia, and began to use murder as a weapon outside the imperial family.

For moralising Romans, Nero's obsession with matters artistic was also abhorrent, since this emperor was interested in carving, painting, singing, poetic composition, lyre-playing and chariot-racing. Seneca and Burrus tried unsuccessfully to conceal his racing activities by confining them to the other side of the Tiber. Nor could they prevent him from organising the Juvenalia, juvenile games, in which the emperor played the lyre and sang.[4] Worse was to come, for by 64 the emperor was appearing on the public stage in Naples,[5] and by 66 and 67 he was engaged in an artistic tour of Greece, participating in all the major festivals.[6]

Equally shocking to Roman sensibilities was Nero's response to the great fire of 64, for the emperor now seized the opportunity to build himself a vast new palace, the Golden House, as part of an enormous complex of buildings and parks occupying some 80 hectares (200 acres) of the city.[7] Suetonius describes it as follows:

It will be sufficient to report this concerning its size and orna-mentation. There was its entrance-hall in which stood a colossal likeness of himself 120 feet high; so great was its width that it held a triple portico a mile long; likewise a lake like a sea, surrounded with buildings in the likeness of cities; different types of countryside with ploughed fields, vineyards, pastures and woods, with a multitude of domestic and wild animals of every kind. In the other parts, all was overlaid with gold and adorned with gems and mother-of-pearl; there were dining-rooms fretted with ivory ceilings, able to turn, so that flowers, and fitted with pipes, so that perfumes could be sprinkled from above. The main dining room was circular so that it could revolve day and night like the firmament; there were baths flowing with sea and sulphur water. When he dedicated the house finished in this way he gave his approval, saying only that now he could begin to live like a human being.

Suetonius *Nero* 31

1. Contexts

For Romans this architectural project proved particularly offensive because so much of the city's space and so much wealth had been lavished on what was essentially a private residence.

But if Nero's rule was both criminal and deeply offensive to traditional morality, it must be acknowledged that these years were notable for literary achievement. It is a striking fact of literary history that the years intervening between Augustus and Nero were relatively barren. By comparison with the Augustan age, the era of Tiberius and Gaius Caligula was not one of great literary achievement. What had happened? Why the apparent lack of literary talent? One reason may be lack of imperial patronage. Unlike Augustus and Nero, Tiberius and Gaius do not seem to have been interested in promoting literature. Another reason may be that writing became a dangerous occupation. Even the relatively benign Augustus had burned the works of the historian Titus Labienus[8] and had banished Ovid to the Black Sea and Cassius Severus to Crete.[9] Tiberius and Gaius proved more oppressive. The history of the Julio-Claudian emperors is one of growing autocracy. Tacitus tells us that the works of the historian Cremutius Cordus were burned by order of Tiberius and that the historian committed suicide.[10] Aelius Saturninus[11] and Sextius Paconianus[12] were put to death by Tiberius for attacking him in their verse. Mamercus Aemilius Scaurus felt obliged to commit suicide after being accused of attacking Tiberius in a tragedy entitled *Atreus*,[13] while an unknown writer of Atellan farce was burned alive under Caligula.[14] In the later years of Claudius and the early years of Nero, however, conditions seem to have improved, perhaps because Claudius was a man with scholarly interests and Nero was an enthusiast for all the arts.

Literature revived to such an extent in the early years of Nero that it is appropriate to speak of a Neronian literary renaissance.[15] There were major achievements in several genres: Persius in satire, Lucan in epic poetry, Calpurnius Siculus in pastoral,[16] Petronius in the novel and, of course, Seneca in philosophy and tragedy.

Seneca

Lucius Annaeus Seneca is a paradox. A man born at the empire's margins in the last years before the common era, he found himself in the 50s and 60s at the very centre of Roman power; though he was famous as a Stoic philosopher, a school which treated riches as being of indifferent value, he was among the wealthiest men in Rome; though renowned as a moral philosopher, he was reputed an adulterer and served one of Rome's most notorious tyrants.

Even in antiquity Seneca generated ambiguous reactions, for on him the historiographical tradition was divided, as Tacitus observed (*Annals* 13.20). For Cassius Dio, a Greek historian of the second and third centuries, Seneca was the paradigmatic hypocrite. After discussing allegations that Seneca had committed adultery with Julia Livilla (Caligula's sister) and Agrippina (Caligula's sister and Nero's mother) Dio offers the following evaluation:

> Not only in this matter but also in many others he was convicted of acting wholly at variance with his philosophy. For while condemning tyranny, he became a tyrant's teacher; and while attacking those who associated with dynasts, he did not refrain from the palace; and while reviling sycophants, he so flattered Messalina and Claudius' ex-slaves that he sent them a book from the island, containing their praises, which he later suppressed through shame; while reproaching the wealthy, he acquired property worth 300,000,000 sesterces.
>
> Cassius Dio 61.10

Dio also claims that Seneca's greed for exorbitant profits was one of the causes of the British rebellion of 61 (62.1). Though denouncing his hypocrisy, Dio is nevertheless willing to acknowledge Seneca's beneficial influence in the early years of Nero's reign, declaring that he and Burrus were the most powerful and most sensible men in Nero's court and that they managed affairs of state as well as they possibly could (61.3).

Tacitus takes a more positive line. The first appearance of

Seneca in the *Annals*, as we have them, is when Agrippina contrives his return from exile in order to assist in the education of her son and to advise in securing the succession (12.8). Once Nero had come to power, Seneca and Burrus are represented by Tacitus as having a positive effect on the young *princeps*, limiting the murderous impulses of Nero and Agrippina, striving to control Nero's vices and restrain his mother's influence (13.2, 5). Even so, Tacitus presents familiar charges against Seneca through the mouth of the loathsome Publius Suillius, charges of adultery and an avarice incompatible with philosophy (13.42). He also records an uncertain role in the murder of Agrippina (14.7, 11) as well as tolerance of Nero's taste for the chariot, the stage and other forms of degradation (14.14). It was the death of Burrus which brought about Seneca's downfall and his retirement from politics (14.52). Once again, criticisms of Seneca's wealth are reported. But they are placed in the mouths of Nero's inferior advisers, while Seneca is described by Tacitus himself as one of virtue's guides (14.52). Seneca's death is described in great detail (15.60-4). Where Dio says that Seneca was involved in a plot to kill Nero (62.24), Tacitus implies that he was an innocent victim of the killings which followed the discovery of Piso's conspiracy. Where Dio claims that Seneca wanted his wife, Paulina, to die with him, Tacitus states that Seneca discouraged her from doing so. Together they slashed their arteries but, at Nero's orders, Paulina's wounds were bound up. Because dying was taking so long, Seneca took hemlock. This too was ineffective and so Seneca died of suffocation. The episode closes with a report that, had the plot been successful, the empire would have been handed over to Seneca as a man of outstanding virtue (15.65). Though showing awareness that aspects of Seneca's involvement in politics were morally problematic, Tacitus gives a relatively positive account of his life.

Seneca was born between 4 and 1 BC in Corduba (modern Cordoba) in the Roman province of Baetica in southern Spain into a family of equestrian rank.[17] He had been taken to Rome before AD 5, for he claimed to have seen the great Asinius Pollio, who died in that year. Seneca entered politics relatively late in life, not holding a magistracy before 33 and entering the Senate late in Tiberius' reign. He was prominent enough as an orator to be criticised by Caligula, who likened his writings to 'sand without lime'.[18] At this time he wrote *Consolation to Marcia*. He was important enough as a politician to be banished to Corsica by Claudius in 41 on the grounds of adultery with Julia Livilla. It was there that he wrote most of *On Anger*. In 49, at the request of Agrippina, Seneca was recalled to become tutor to the twelve-year-old Nero.

After Nero's accession in 54, it fell to Seneca, who held no official position, and to Burrus, who was prefect of the praetorian guard, to watch over the young emperor. Both Tacitus and Dio report that Seneca, together with Burrus, was responsible for a period of good government early in Nero's reign.

Why are the historians' evaluations of Seneca's role at this time as positive as they are? First of all, a primary aim of Seneca and Burrus seems to have been to limit Agrippina's control over her son. Thus Seneca averted the spectacle of a woman exercising power when Agrippina attempted to join Nero at a reception for the Armenian ambassadors.[19] He also contrived concealment from his mother of the emperor's affair with Acte.[20] Secondly, Seneca and Burrus were seen as responsible for making good appointments, for selecting, for example, Corbulo for the war against Parthia and Otho for the governorship of Lusitania.[21] Thirdly, during this period Nero at least gave the impression of fulfilling his accession promises, in particular his promise to respect the Senate's role in government. Thus Claudius' abuses of the emperor's judicial powers were removed and the role of imperial ex-slaves in government was reduced. Even the coinage suggested respect for senatorial participation in government and no senator was accused of treason during the ascendancy of Seneca and Burrus.[22]

However, involvement with Nero inevitably led to moral compromise. Seneca was obliged to acquiesce in the murder of Britannicus, even praising Nero for guiltlessness some nine months later.[23] And after Nero's bungled attempt at murdering

Agrippina, Seneca became implicated in her death,[24] eventually having the task of writing a message to the Senate announcing her doom in terms which implied that she had been plotting against Nero's life.[25]

The death of Burrus in 62 led to a weakening of Seneca's position and a request for retirement from politics. Although the request was denied, Seneca effectively withdrew from public life.[26] After the fire of Rome in 64, Seneca asked for permission to leave Rome altogether.[27] When this was refused, Seneca feigned illness and declined to leave his bedroom, living on wild fruits and water. This period of retirement was prolific, for at this time Seneca composed the *Natural Questions*, one hundred and twenty-four *Letters to Lucilius*, and, most probably, two tragedies, *Thyestes* and *Phoenician Women*.[28]

The date of *Thyestes*

Lack of external evidence makes it impossible to date Seneca's tragedies with absolute confidence or precision. However, parodies of *Hercules* and *Trojan Women* in Seneca's skit on the death of Claudius, suggest (but only suggest) that those plays were written before AD 54.[29] In addition, the metrical and other arguments of Fitch,[30] which have been endorsed by significant philologists,[31] seem to offer sure grounds for dividing the corpus into three groups, an early group comprising *Agamemnon*, *Phaedra* and *Oedipus*, a middle group consisting of *Medea*, *Trojan Women* and *Hercules*, and a late group containing *Thyestes* and *Phoenissae* and for accepting that the plays were composed over a long period of time.[32] In addition, the Romanised world of *Thyestes* seems to allude to the reign of Nero, particularly the mention of bestowing diadems on client kings at 599-606, which suggests Nero's installation of Tigranes on the throne of Armenia in AD 60,[33] and the reference to the Alani at 629f., who were pressing on the borders of Moesia in the 60s.[34] Moreover, the close relationship between *Thyestes* and *On Mercy* suggests that the play is later than the treatise, which is securely dated to 55 or 56. As both Tarrant and Nisbet suggest, a date in the early 60s seems likely for *Thyestes*, the most likely period being Seneca's withdrawal from public life, 62-65.[35] *Thyestes* will then embody Seneca's reflections upon his experiences during the first decade of Nero's reign.

Roman tragedy

Under the republic Roman tragic drama was associated with major religious festivals sponsored by the Roman state which were held regularly throughout the year. Theatrical performances were associated with the *ludi Megalenses* (early April), the *ludi Cereales* (late April), the *ludi Florales* (early May), the *ludi Apollinares* (July), the *ludi Romani* (September) and the *ludi Plebeii* (November). It has been calculated that in the 180s BC, when both Plautus and Ennius were active, there were about fourteen official days available for dramatic performances.[36] In addition dramatic performances were associated with celebrations held in honour of some special event, to celebrate a military success or to honour the spirit of a deceased noble. These festivals were believed to have been introduced to Rome from Etruria in 364, but it was not until 240 BC that an adaptation of an Athenian play found its way onto the Roman stage. After 240, performances of classics of the Athenian tragic stage in Latin versions became regular at Rome.

The author of this first Latin tragedy was Livius Andronicus, an ex-slave, who was also the author of the Latin version of Homer's *Odyssey*. Under the republic the four best known authors of tragic dramas were Naevius (who died around 200), Ennius (239-169), Pacuvius (220 – c. 131) and Accius (170 – c. 86). Both Naevius and Ennius also composed comedies, whereas Pacuvius and Accius devoted themselves exclusively to the tragic stage. All four composed plays on Roman historical themes (*fabulae praetextae*) as well as on themes drawn from Greek mythology. Of the four Accius seems to have been the most popular in the late republic, his plays being revived on a number of occasions. Unfortunately none of the works of these authors has survived complete.

1. Contexts

Little is known about the manner of performance of tragedy under the republic. The Latin poets seem to have limited the role of the Chorus. One factor in this may have been the restriction of the Chorus to the stage area, the area used by the actors. Hence the elaborate singing and dancing characteristic of fifth-century tragedy would have been impossible. They also pruned the metrical variety of the choral odes. We do know that Roman actors wore the tragic mask (Cicero *De Oratore* 3.221), robe and buskins. From Horace's *Art of Poetry* we learn that the five-act structure had become standard (189f.) and that it was still conventional that any tragedy could be performed by no more than three actors (192).

All theatres in Rome were temporary wooden structures until the building of the theatre of Pompey (55 BC). This theatre was radically different in conception from the Greek theatres of the fifth and fourth centuries. Unlike them it was a free-standing structure in which the stage-building, the semi-circular orchestra and two-tiered auditorium enclosed a unified space. In terms of later theatres Pompey's was eccentric in that it incorporated a temple of Venus in the auditorium. The next theatres to be built in Rome were those of Balbus (13 BC) and Marcellus (11 BC). This latter theatre, begun by Julius Caesar and completed by Augustus and dedicated to the memory of his nephew, became the prototype for theatres throughout the empire. Apart from their physical remains, our main source of knowledge concerning theatrical buildings is Vitruvius, an architectural writer of the Augustan age. From Vitruvius we learn that the stage in a Roman theatre was wider than that of the Greeks, because all actors played their part on the stage, that the space in the orchestra was allotted to the seating of senators and that the stage building consisted of a palace with three sets of doors, those on the right and the left being for the entrances of strangers (*On Architecture* 5.6).

As far as we can tell from the surviving evidence, the most popular mythological theme for Roman tragedy was that of Atreus and Thyestes. Thus plays entitled *Atreus* are recorded as having been written by Accius, Publius Pomponius Secundus,

Aemilius Scaurus and Rubrenus Lappa, while plays entitled *Thyestes* are attributed to Ennius, Varius, Cassius, Gracchus, Curiatius Maternus, Ligurinus and Bassus.[37] Of all these plays substantial fragments survive of only two, Ennius' *Thyestes* (169 BC) and Accius' *Atreus* (*c.* 135 BC).[38]

Ennius was one of the great figures of the earliest phase of Roman literature, being the author of a major epic on Rome's history, the *Annales*, satires and comedies as well as tragedies. *Thyestes* was Ennius' last play, produced in the last year of his life.[39] Roughly 25 verses survive from this play.[40] Ennius' play was very different from Seneca's, for it dramatised later events. Set in the court of Thesprotus, Ennius' *Thyestes* included Thyestes' rape of his daughter Pelopia and her marriage to Atreus.[41]

Accius was perhaps the most widely admired of the republican tragedians, Velleius Paterculus declaring that *in Accio circaque eum Romana tragoedia est* ('Roman tragedy is in Accius and around him', 1.17). His play, *Atreus*, seems to have affinities with Seneca's *Thyestes*.[42] It contained a scene, apparently foreshadowing Act 2, in which Atreus outlined his plans to crush his brother, including the infamous line: *oderint dum metuant* ('let them hate, as long as they fear'). Atreus also showed himself concerned with matters of heredity, for he is concerned about Aerope's adultery and the paternity of his sons. The play also included Atreus' instructions concerning the feast, the flight of the sun, a messenger's description of the killing and cooking of the children, a representation of Thyestes' distress and a debate between the two brothers. Seneca's suggestion in *On Anger*,[43] that the play is what you would expect from the time of Sulla, implies that Accius' play too was concerned with the nature of tyranny.

2

Performance History

Albeit when first I undertoke the translation of this present Tragœdy, I minded nothing lesse, than that any tyme thus rudely transformed it shoulde come into the Printers hands. For I to none other ende removed him, from his naturall and lofty style, to our corrupt and base, or as some men (but untruly) affyrme it, most barbarous Language: but onely to satisfy the instant requests of a few my familiar friends, who thought to have put it to the very same use, that *Seneca* himselfe in his Invention pretended: Which was by the tragicall and Pompous showe upon Stage, to admonish all men of their fickle estates ...

> Alexander Neville, Preface to translation
> of Seneca's *Oedipus* (1563).[1]

The best actors in the world, either for tragedy, comedy ... Seneca cannot be too heavy nor Plautus too light.

> Polonius in Shakespeare, *Hamlet* (1600)[2]

Whether a writer expected his play to be played or not is irrelevant, the point is whether it is playable.

> T.S. Eliot, 'Seneca in Elizabethan Translation' (1927)[3]

Nor do I suppose that there is a strong dramatic link with the closet drama of Seneca, whose frozen horrors are designed for static declamation and can have offered little or nothing to professional actors or to the audiences who went along for the excitement of quick-fire action and surprise.

> G.K. Hunter (1986)[4]

Performance or recitation drama?

One of the most contentious issues concerning Seneca's tragedies is whether they were written for stage performance. The Senecan texts look remarkably like the texts of other ancient tragedies. On the first page we find a list of characters and a setting. As we progress we see that speeches are assigned to different characters and that the work is punctuated by passages in lyric verse attributed to a chorus. Characters soliloquise or debate with each other; actions are both represented and reported. We do not see stage directions, but these, as always in ancient texts, are implied rather than explicitly stated. Apart from its language, the text of *Thyestes* differs in no significant way from the text of a Greek tragedy, for *Thyestes* possesses all the textual markers of performance drama that we expect to find when dealing with works from the ancient world.

Consequently it is not surprising that for scholars and dramatists of the Elizabethan age Seneca was an author whose plays were plainly written for the stage: Alexander Neville tells us that his translation of Seneca's *Oedipus* resembles the original in being written for performance, not publication, while Polonius' reference to Senecan tragedy, part of his eulogy of a company of itinerant actors, enables us to infer that England's greatest dramatist held the same opinion. And yet nowadays some think otherwise.

Why is it that Seneca's tragedies seem to some contemporary scholars of Roman and English literature incapable of stage performance? Why are they assigned to the category of 'recitation' or 'closet' drama?

Perhaps the most common reason is that adduced by Hunter: the plays are said to be static, lacking in action, and therefore more appropriate to presentation by a single speaker than to stage production.[5] But judgements of this kind very much depend on one's perspective. To contemporary spectators and readers accustomed to the kind of sensational action we find in Shakespeare or in the movies, Seneca may seem static. But so too will Aeschylus and Racine. And yet the performability of their plays, for good and obvious reasons, remains unquestioned.

What would Hunter make of Aeschylus' greatest surviving play, *Agamemnon*? Here the drama consists almost entirely of lengthy speeches and extended choral odes.[6] Apart from entrances and exits, the play holds very little action. It begins with the Watchman's speech, after which Clytemnestra enters in order to inform the Chorus of Troy's capture. Next the herald enters to announce Agamemnon's imminent arrival. Agamemnon now enters with Cassandra and is welcomed by Clytemnestra. It is only now that we have significant action: Agamemnon trampling on the tapestries as he enters the palace. This is followed by the confrontation between Cassandra and Clytemnestra, Cassandra's prophecy of her own and Agamemnon's death and the sound of Agamemnon's death cries from within the palace. Next Clytemnestra and Aegisthus make a dramatically powerful entry, standing over the bodies of Agamemnon and Cassandra. This is followed by a debate between Clytemnestra and the Chorus and the entry of Aegisthus with armed men. By the standards of Shakespeare or the movies, Aeschylus' play is static. Here is no exciting quick-fire action or surprise of the kind that Hunter wants. And yet we know that the play was a highly successful theatrical piece in the fifth century BC and that it has been performed to great acclaim in our own time. The complaint by Hunter and other scholars of Elizabethan drama that Senecan tragedy is static reveals not the unperformability of Senecan tragedy, but their lack of sympathy for tragedy in the classical tradition.

By comparison with Aeschylus' *Agamemnon*, *Thyestes* is action-packed. To begin with, there are fewer and briefer choral odes. The play begins with an unnamed Fury[7] dragging the ghost of Tantalus from his underworld punishment towards the palace at Argos so that he can reactivate the family's innate thirst for blood. We see Tantalus attempting to escape, trying to block the Fury's entry into the house, resisting until the Fury lashes him into submission. Tantalus then enters the house and is dismissed. Act 2 presents Atreus, ruler of Argos, whipping himself into a frenzy of anger and hatred against his brother, Thyestes. We see Atreus plotting his revenge, planning a false reconciliation and debating with his Minister. Act 3 presents Thyestes' entry in rags, his encounter with and seduction by Atreus, his assumption of crown and royal robes. Act 4 is taken up with a powerful narrative, the Messenger's report of Atreus' killing and cooking of Thyestes' children and of their consumption by their father. Act 5 presents Atreus' victorious entry, the revelation of the belching Thyestes, his drunken song, and the disclosure of the children's heads. By ancient standards, *Thyestes* is anything but static.

But behind Hunter's view there is an assumption that needs to be resisted, the view that speech unaccompanied by vigorous action is intrinsically undramatic. It is not the length of a speech that is important, but its quality. Although Elizabethan dramatists might learn little from Seneca about quick-fire action and surprise, there was much to learn about dramatic irony, about effective scene construction, about the creation of coherent dramatic structures and, above all, about the use of rhetoric, for their dramas are no less rhetorical than his.

A second major objection to the performability of Senecan drama is the argument that events occur in Senecan tragedy which are incapable of being staged. Thus Hutchinson tells us that 'physical events in Seneca's plays are often wildly unreal', citing the example of *Oedipus* 371-80, the inspection of the entrails of a sacrificial beast, as a passage which is unplayable.[8] This is akin to believing 'that Indians in Westerns are really shot',[9] for to claim that events of this kind cannot be staged is to ignore the role of convention in theatrical production. It is also to ignore the fact that Seneca's *Oedipus* has been successfully performed in modern times. In particular, Peter Brook's 1968 production at the National Theatre in London was so important a theatrical event that it was commemorated with a fresh production in 1988 by Donald Sumpter at the Almeida.[10] Clearly the scene's difficulties are not insurmountable.

More telling than the weakness of arguments against playability is the fact that certain episodes in Senecan tragedy only

make sense if they are performed before an audience of spectators.[11] The treatment of the Chorus in *Thyestes* is a case in
point. In Act 2 Atreus reveals to his Minister his true plans, in
particular the fact that he proposes to lure his brother to Argos
in order to take his revenge. However, the Chorus which follows
seems quite unfamiliar with these events. After line 335 they
sing their second ode. Their opening words are, superficially at
least, surprising (336-8):

> tandem regia nobilis,
> antiqui genus Inachi
> fratrum composuit minas.

> At last the royal house, the family of ancient Inachus, has settled
> the strife of brothers.

The words are surprising, because the audience knows them to
be false. Sutton[12] attempted to resolve the difficulty posed by
these lines by deleting them, a solution first proposed by Richter.
However, this textual emendation does not resolve the contra-
diction, for the Chorus proves equally ignorant of the events of
Act 2 in their third ode as well (546-59). Otherwise they could
not interpret the apparent reconciliation of Act 3 as resulting
from *pietas* (549). Editorial surgery is not the solution.

But if we accept that Seneca followed Hellenistic and Roman,
as opposed to fifth-century Greek, practice, and that a Senecan
chorus may or may not be present during an act,[13] the problem
is more apparent than real. It is not difficult for us, if we are an
audience in a theatre, to grasp what has taken place. Having
seen that the Chorus-members were absent during Act 2, we
can deduce that they have heard and believed reports of the
proposed reconciliation between the two brothers. We know,
however, from their visible absence from the stage in Act 2, that
they were not privy to Atreus' true plans. The optimistic
opening to Ode 2 will cause an attentive audience of spectators
no surprise at all.

Since Zwierlein's[14] classic statement of the case for recitation
drama in 1966, his position has steadily been losing ground in

the English-speaking world.[15] In 1969 Walker declared that the book's 'effect on the present reviewer was to make what previously seemed a doubtful issue into one of extreme probability against Zwierlein's view'.[16]

Some Senecan scholars now accept that Seneca wrote with either the public or private stage in mind. Thus Sutton argues for public performance,[17] while Calder favours private performance[18] and Boyle,[19] whose translations of *Phaedra* and *Troades* were actually written for the stage,[20] supports stage production whether public or private.[21]

Others, though reluctant to believe that Seneca wrote with performance in mind, acknowledge the plays' undeniable dramatic qualities. Thus Hine, though arguing that 'in the debate about staging neither side can deliver a knock-out blow to the other', accepts that 'perhaps any reading or hearing of the play will be enriched by making the effort to imagine it being performed',[22] while Tarrant, having accepted the Zwierlein position without qualification in his 1976 edition of *Agamemnon*,[23] acknowledged in his 1985 edition of *Thyestes* that Senecan rhetoric possesses 'a strong theatrical flavor'[24] and, while conceding that the plays may actually have been performed in Seneca's own lifetime,[25] continued to believe that 'Seneca conceived his plays without regard for the restraints of theatrical production'.[26] Similarly, Coffey argues that 'though Seneca's primary intention was to provide a vehicle for animated recitation or declamation in which the audience was persuaded to share the illusion of an enacted drama, the possibility that his plays were performed in whole or part should not be excluded'.[27]

That a sea-change has taken place in the English-speaking world is confirmed by the publication of Harrison's *Seneca in Performance*,[28] a collection of papers deriving from a combined conference on Senecan tragedy and production of *Trojan Women* held in Cincinnati in 1998. Perhaps not surprisingly, those most closely associated with the dramatic performance – Frederick Ahl,[29] whose translation was used, and Gyllian Raby,[30] the play's director – were unambiguous supporters of stage performance, but so too were C.W. Marshall, who contributed an important essay on theatrical aspects of Seneca's handling of the Chorus in *Troades*[31] and George W.M. Harrison, who discussed the physical setting for ancient performances. Even former supporters of the 'recitation-drama theory' offered 'partial recantations',[32] with Fitch arguing that some scenes were written with staging in mind and that some were not, his central examples being Act 5 of *Thyestes* for theatrical power and of the sacrifice-scene in *Oedipus* for unperformability.[33] Fantham endorsed that position, continuing to insist that 'all stage-action must be verbally signalled', and then offered four pages of stage-directions for an ideal performance of *Trojan Women*.[34]

Dupont, having been involved in major French productions of Senecan tragedy, including *Thyestes*,[35] has argued that the question is wrongly posed. She claims that where some of our contemporaries see verbosity, the Romans saw eloquence and the pleasure of orality and that 'verbosity' and 'lengthy monologues' were an intrinsic part of all Roman tragedy. Thus the question 'is Seneca playable?' breaks down into two questions: 'is Roman tragedy playable in current conditions?' and 'did Seneca write "genuine" Roman tragedies?'. Dupont holds that in both cases the answer is 'yes'. She argues that, as an amateur tragedian, Seneca in fact wrote for the recitation hall and that writing for the recitation hall entailed conformity to the rules of the tragic stage. Thus she concludes:

> It is entertaining to state finally that the two sides of the debate are both right, for Seneca is a genuine dramatic poet, having written real tragedies, precisely because he intended them for public reading.[36]

Thus Dupont collapses the distinction between recitation and performance drama by arguing that Seneca wrote for the recitation hall, and that that entailed writing in accordance with the rules of the tragic stage. Although Dupont's compromise is intriguing, it should be noted that there is no necessary connection between amateur tragedian and recitation hall, for Tacitus tells us that Pomponius Secundus, an ex-consul, wrote for the stage (*quod in Publium Pomponium consularem – is carmina scaenae dabat*: *Annals* 11.13).

It must be admitted that there is no evidence for actual stage performance of *Thyestes* or other Senecan tragedies in antiquity. Consequently, Hine is right, in one sense, to say that the problem is insoluble. However, what is at stake here is not so much Seneca's intentions, as the nature of the texts before us. As T.S. Eliot said, 'whether a writer expected his play to be played or not is irrelevant, the point is whether it is playable'.[37] And, in my view, there is no doubt that Seneca's tragedies are as playable as any other dramatic scripts which have come down to us from classical antiquity. The first point to note, as Herington observed, is 'that Senecan dramatic verse is designed, no less than the verse of Marlowe or Racine, for its effect on the ear, not on the eye; and that effect is shattering'.[38] Seneca writes superbly speakable verse. Secondly, again as Herington points out, some Senecan passages demand more than one speaker. Herington quotes *Medea* 168-71:

> *Nut.* rex est timendus. *Me.* rex meus fuerat pater.
> *Nut.* non metuis arma? *Me.* sint licet terra edita.
> *Nut.* moriere. *Me.* cupio. *Nut.* profuge. *Me.* paenituit fugae.
> *Nut.* Medea – *Me.* fiam. *Nut.* mater es. *Me.* cui sim uides.

> *Nurse*: The king must be feared. *Med.*: My father was a king.
> *Nurse*: Do you not fear weapons? *Med.*: Not even if they are
> sprung from earth.
> *Nurse*: You will die. *Med.*: I long to. *Nurse*: Flee. *Med.*: I regret
> flight.
> *Nurse*: Medea – *Med.*: I will become. *Nurse*: You are a mother.
> *Med.*: You see by whom.

Herington then asks: 'What can a *single* reciter make of that?'. He rightly concludes that these are lines which require more than one speaker. How would a single actor cope with the last two lines, lines in which each of two speakers speaks twice?[39]

Seneca's tragedies are not merely playable: they demand performance upon the stage.[40]

Types of tragic performance

What kinds of performance were available to a Roman dramatist of the first century AD? Our evidence concerning theatrical performances under the empire is limited. There were three kinds of tragic performance. First, we know that dramatists continued to write tragedies with a view to full-scale theatrical performance. Pomponius Secundus, for example, a tragedian highly admired by Tacitus and Quintilian, certainly composed for the public stage.[41] Secondly, we also have evidence for a more private kind of dramatic performance, performances taking place in the homes of wealthy individuals. Pliny[42] chides a friend who failed to accept a dinner invitation on the grounds that he might have heard, among other things, a performance by comic actors. Plutarch records that performances by the Greek comic poet Menander were popular at Roman dinner parties and that slave actors performed Platonic dialogues under similar circumstances.[43] Thirdly, we know that some tragedies were composed which were not intended for the stage. The *Medea* of Ovid (this has not survived) may be an example.[44] Such works were intended for private reading or for public recitation. *Thyestes* and the other Senecan tragedies belong, in my view, to either or both of the first two categories.

Twentieth-century performances of *Thyestes*

Any production of *Thyestes* faces one insuperable problem from the beginning: it's not actually a terribly good play. It's badly paced (for a start, it's too short) and gory rather than horrific ....
    Antony G. Keen, 'Review: Lucius Annaeus Seneca's Thyestes'

Seneca ... places human beings face to face with themselves, haunted by their past, setting out the keys to their future. His theatre is transparent, clear-sighted, humane.
    Olivier Schmitt, 'Thyeste à Nanterre-Amandiers'

That *Thyestes* and other Senecan tragedies were intended for performance seems confirmed by the fact that the plays have been so often performed in modern times. We know, for example, that they were performed in the fifteenth and sixteenth centuries: we have evidence of Renaissance productions of *Medea, Oedipus, Phaedra, Thyestes* and *Trojan Women* in England, Germany and Italy.[45] Since we know little about these productions beyond the fact of their having taken place, I will concentrate on performances associated with the twentieth-century revival of interest in Senecan drama.

The first twentieth-century production of *Thyestes* took place on 6 February 1953, at the Teatro Valle in Rome.[46] It was directed by Vittorio Gassman and Luigi Squarzina, with Gassman as Atreus and Annibale Ninchi as Thyestes in a translation by Gassman. According to Squarzina, the production was important not only as the first modern performance of Seneca, but as an attempt to create a Theatre of Cruelty in the manner of Antonin Artaud.[47]

Gassman's approach to staging *Thyestes* was to take risks. To underline the horrific aspects of the Senecan text, the designer Lete Luzzati eschewed a conventional, quasi-classical staging, avoiding an archaeological or historical approach, preferring to suggest an archaic world of primordial passions. The stage was decked with totem-like symbols, adapted from Aegean and Near Eastern iconography. To left and right were huge zoomorphic thrones. Atreus and Thyestes wore stiff tunics, intended to suggest both priest and warrior, while supernatural characters wore tights, the furies having snake-hair and wings and Tantalus wearing a black net. The Chorus, consisting of just one person, wore a white woollen tunic bordered in black.

In Act 1 Gassman attempted to create an atmosphere of gloom in a space ambiguous between hell and the Argive palace, a region inhabited by the furies and the damned. For him the scene's dynamic centre was Tantalus' resistance to the Fury's command and the overwhelming force which compels his obedience. The stage was then lit, four soldiers of Atreus entered and then the one-man Chorus. Gassman viewed the Chorus, not as an embodiment of the civic community, as in Greek tragedy, but as an artisan whose conscience, voice and thought are those of Seneca. In Act 2 Atreus entered in quasi-priestly costume. The Minister he saw as a shifty man, fat, bald and timid. Here too Gassman saw autobiographical references, with the Minister being reminiscent of Seneca as Nero's tutor and counsellor, a Seneca deluded in his hope of controlling and softening the tyrant. As for Thyestes, Gassman stressed that the actor playing this role should avoid making him a victim so as not to destroy the play's opposition between two forces and two types of evil, both condemned by the poet and the Chorus. Thyestes and his sons entered in wretched clothes. Here dramatic tension arises from the sons' naïve confidence and the father's supreme diffidence. For the encounter between the brothers Gassman brought on Atreus' children, Agamemnon and Menelaus, who began to play with their cousins, with the little ones playing light-heartedly, the older ones playing with instinctive rivalry. Atreus and Thyestes embraced, Thyestes knelt down until raised by his brother. Thyestes then sat on the throne. The scene closed with Thyestes being dressed as priest-king and Atreus leading away his children.

For the Messenger in Act 4, Gassman used the ghost of Tantalus, justifying this move by arguing that this messenger was more abstract than the messengers of classical tragedy, that there were no human witnesses to Atreus' crimes and, more importantly, that it drew attention to the predestined, hereditary aspects of the brothers' actions. The final choral ode presented the greatest problems, for in Gassman's view it deals with profound issues, but in a manner more rhetorical than theatrical. On the other hand, it does create a valuable pause between the Messenger's narrative and Atreus' entry. As for the climactic scene, Gassman wrote as follows:

> It is necessary to confront directly, without second thoughts, without caution, the possible ridicule of 'heads cut off', of 'hands lopped', of 'lifeblood': the grotesque, the macabre, the excessive, which could provoke a reaction in the plot of a bourgeois drama, are here the equivalent of an approximation to tragic emotion.[48]

According to Concetto Marchesi, the final scene worked particularly well, largely because of Ninchi's performance as
Thyestes, especially his handling of Thyestes' response to the
revelation of his children's heads.[49]

Despite the novelty of the achievement and despite
Gassman's theatrical brilliance, the public response to this first
modern production of *Thyestes* seems to have been largely nega-
tive. Concetto Marchesi, writing in *Rinascita*, blamed Gassman
for the weaknesses of the performance:

> Gassman's daring attempt has nevertheless demonstrated that
> with more respect for the word and its expressive value, with
> more perspicacity and decisiveness in blackouts, with more
> emphasis on truly dramatic essentials, with less love of the
> grotesque in staging, with a wise preference for silence over noise
> and with a more thoughtful observation of the appropriate tone
> of voice and gesture, Senecan tragedy could take life on the stage
> of the modern theatre.[50]

Even more pointedly Marchesi commented, 'Gassman's Atreus
almost always shouts', while Pandolfi spoke of 'Gassman's
paroxysm', observing that the cry of blood for blood can be
expressed in ways other than shouting.[51] Despite the seeming
lack of popular and critical success, Gassman directed *Thyestes*
once more in 1960.

It was not until the 1970s that a British production of
Thyestes took the stage. In October and November 1975 David
Hayman directed *Thyestes* for the Citizens Theatre in
Glasgow,[52] using Watling's translation.[53] Hayman's production
was subsidised by the Scottish Arts Council's support for 'new
or rarely performed work'. Hayman clearly thought the play
'rarely performed' for good reason, for his programme quoted
without comment Schlegel's judgement that Seneca's plays are
'barren of all theatrical effect'. Reaction to the play was very
much divided. However, certain things are clear. Hayman
brought his experience of life in Kenya to the text and staged
the play as if the events had taken place among an African tribe.

The actors were virtually naked and painted black. The performances of the principal actors generated diverse reactions, with Christopher Small, writing in the *Glasgow Herald*, declaring that Gerard Murphy, the production's Atreus, bellowed and galumphed about the stage, and that Rupert Frazer, as Thyestes, though more restrained, adopted a 'Sambo accent'. By contrast, George Bruce, writing in the *Sunday Times*, claimed that 'the ecstasies and anguishes of the intense performances of Gerard Murphy as Atreus and Rupert Frazer as Thyestes find powerful expression'. Opinion also differed as to the relative merits of Hayman's and Seneca's contributions to the performance. The *Glasgow Herald* expressed the desire to see another production of the play, though 'with a little more taste and judgment' and with a director other than Hayman in control, while the *Sunday Times* claimed that 'had Mr Hayman simply been faithful to Seneca, we should have had only a bloody rhetorical tragedy'.

It was not until the 1980s that *Thyestes* was produced in the United States.[54] In 1987 (28-30 April) Panagiotis Agapitos directed *Thyestes* in a translation by Richard Tarrant at the Agassiz Theatre, Harvard College.[55] The emphasis in this production was on disjointedness, for Agapitos aimed to stress the incongruence of word and action, myth and history, Greek and Roman. Consequently he presented the play 'as a rehearsal of a "Roman-costume" *Thyestes*'. Roles were assigned to the various characters to demonstrate the relations between them, with, for example, the director also playing Atreus and the same actor playing the shade of Tantalus in Act 1 and the young Tantalus in Act 3. The choral odes were recited in Latin 'in order to underline the reversal of order by alienating the Chorus linguistically from the main body of the play'. Each performance was accompanied by music (piano and percussion) freshly improvised for each performance.

The 1990s were remarkable years in the performance history of *Thyestes*, for the play was performed in several European cities: Milan and Segesta in 1991, Manchester and London in 1994, Paris in 1995 and 1999, and Rome in 1998.[56]

However, the decade began badly. In April 1991 Antonio Syxty staged *Thyestes* in a translation by Raul Montanari at the Teatro Out Off in Milan.[57] Reviewing the play for *Corriere della Sera*, Giovanni Raboni claimed that he was grateful to Syxty for sending him back to Seneca's text and 'its still living greatness'. He was not, however, grateful to Syxty for his theatrical stunts. Syxty surprised his audience by having all parts played by women. There were five actors, all dressed in jacket, bra and miniskirt, who seemed to have come from a television commercial or a sadomasochistic film. Further, at the beginning of the play the actors wore Mickey Mouse masks. Equally striking was some of the stage business: this included dance, rolling on the ground, pretending to be on the phone, simulating lesbian sex and seeming to hold up the décor while snoring. Perhaps not surprisingly, Raboni considered that all this was a distraction from the text, rather than an attempt to bring it to life. Nevertheless Raboni found praise for the actors and the translator, if not the director.[58]

Of much greater theatrical power and dramatic significance was the production included in INDA's (Istituzione Nazionale del Drama Antico) sixth summer festival of ancient drama held in 1991 at the ancient theatre of Segesta in Sicily.[59] For this production the director was Walter Pagliaro and the play was translated by members of the INDA drama school under the direction of Giusto Picone. Perhaps not surprisingly, the acting space, occupying both the ancient stage and orchestra, took the form of combined rectangle and semicircle. The centre of the acting space was occupied by an area delimited by thrones and containing a floor with a labyrinthine pattern surrounding a mirror-like surface. In front of this was a rectangular subterranean opening which functioned as an entrance from the underworld for the Fury in Act 1 and as an entrance from the palace for Thyestes in Act 5.

Perhaps the most obvious disadvantage of using an ancient theatre for the production of a play whose last act takes place in darkness is the fact that ancient theatres are open to sky and sun. This difficulty was overcome by having the performance begin in the latter part of the day and end in natural darkness. The problem of visibility in Act 5 was solved by judicious use of lighting, particularly an eerie red glow which seemed to issue from the subterranean opening. Bathed in this light, the contest between Atreus and Thyestes in their final scene was one of explosive impact.

Although the production avoided the usual classical clichés, it conformed in significant ways to ancient norms. Thus the Chorus of three men entered and exited with the freedom we associate with Roman tragedy, being either absent or wholly disengaged from the stage-action in Acts 1, 2, 3 and 5, but present to hear the Messenger's speech in Act 4. The most significant props were those suggested by the text: a golden cup, a royal robe and garland. The mirror-like surface was used to particular effect in Atreus' scene of self-exhortation at the beginning of Act 2. But the production's greatest strength was its powerful acting, for it employed some of Italy's best known stage and cinema actors: Maurizio Gueli as Tantalus' ghost, Giuseppe Pambieri as Atreus, Virginio Gazzolo as Thyestes and Luciano Virgilio as the Messenger.

Equally significant was the British production which took place on 1-4 June, at The Green Room in Manchester, and on 7-10 June at The Royal Court Theatre in London. The play was translated by Caryl Churchill, one of Britain's most eminent dramatists, and directed by James Macdonald. The play was presented in modern dress and employed various multimedia devices (video camera, television screens). The production was presented as a precursor to both *Hamlet* and *Reservoir Dogs*.

Churchill's translation was praised by reviewers. Her version makes little attempt to convey the flavour of Senecan rhetoric, for Churchill employs a line considerably shorter than Seneca's iambic trimeter and breaks down Senecan periods into short, snappy sentences. She has also pared back mythological allusions, presumably in the belief that they would prove impenetrable to modern audiences. However, her rendering is otherwise accurate, vigorous and lively.

The production was high-tech and modern dress.[60] The audience, arriving to the sound of liquids pouring and tearing metal, entered past two small rooms, one containing a dining table with a painted meal and a video camera pointing at it, the other with the crouched one-man Chorus. Upon entering, the audience confronted a number of large monitors displaying shots of the table, Atreus looking out a window and Hades. The monitors were used throughout the play so that Atreus could watch his brother's approach to Argos and his consumption of his sons. The function of the cameras clearly was, as Paul Taylor pointed out, to 'serve as accusing symbols of our modern voyeuristic fascination with violence, and of our dislocation from it'.[61] If we remember that ancient Romans were as much bound up in a culture of violent spectacle as we are, for they could view the mangling of human flesh in the city's amphitheatres, then the video screen seems apt metaphor for the arena.

Despite Eliot's dictum that 'his characters all seem to speak with the same voice, and at the top of it',[62] the director, James Macdonald, was clearly aiming at understatement. John Gross put it like this: 'Ewan Stewart as Thyestes is soft-spoken, almost restrained, when he learns what has been done to him – until the full horror dawns, and he cries out that he will break his chest by beating it. But he calms down again for his final curse: yet one more example, always assuming you have the requisite power, of how much it pays to avoid bombast.'[63] Irving Wardle noted that the actors 'seldom raise their voices'.[64] Seneca's rhetoric is so effective and the play's action is so powerful that rant and bombast are not appropriate to *Thyestes*.

Study of the play's reviews is instructive. While reviews written by scholars were laden with abuse, accounts by journalists were, for the most part, less prejudiced. Thus Edith Hall's claim in the *Times Literary Supplement* that Senecan tragedy is 'staggeringly inert, verbose, unsuggestive of stage action and stubbornly resistant to theatrical realization'[65] is an admission of bias rather than a statement of fact. In similar fashion, when Antony Keen began his review in *Didaskalia* with the words 'any production of *Thyestes* faces one insuperable problem from the beginning: it's not actually a terribly good play',[66] he was more instructive about the nature of the article to follow than about the play.

By contrast, journalists writing for the general public, though sometimes revealing their awareness of handbook commonplaces, were more open-minded. Some made little effort to comprehend: 'just a lot of Scotsmen in suits shouting in a bare room, with a curly-wigged man in a red frock moaning' wrote Robin Thornber in the *Guardian*. By contrast, Michael Coveney in the *Observer*, though aware that 'Seneca's tragedies may not have been intended for performance', acknowledged that 'a reasonable case for his dramaturgical significance is also entered',[67] while Paul Taylor in the *Independent* reflected upon the fact that '*Thyestes* is a play which wonders volubly whether there are any limits to the cruelty human beings will inflict on each other'.[68] Equally thoughtful were John Gross (*Sunday Telegraph*), who recognised that 'her [Churchill's] version constantly prompts thoughts not just of literary fantasies, but of the real world – of the ethics of revenge, of the latest reports from Rwanda, of what has happened in its time on all five continents' and Irving Wardle (*Independent on Sunday*) who called the production 'cold-bloodedly illuminating'.[69] It seems that, for the most part, critics who did not 'know' that Senecan tragedy was worthless responded positively to Macdonald's production.

In France, by contrast, questions of the theatricality and the value of Senecan tragedy were not raised.[70] *Thyestes* was performed in Paris in 1995 as part of a cycle of productions of all Seneca's tragedies.[71] *Thyestes*, along with *Trojan Women* and *Agamemnon*, was directed by Adel Hakim at the Théâtre des Quartiers d'Ivry in October and November, with the three plays being presented separately during the week and as a trilogy on weekends, the trilogy lasting for about six hours.[72] The translation was by a well-known classical scholar, Florence Dupont, who had already declared in 1985 that 'Seneca's theatricality is a theatricality of spectacle where words are not enough'.[73]

This production lacked the high-tech wizardry of the London production, but it too was in modern dress. At the back of the stage for all three plays was a partly-ruined wall with three entrances; in the centre was a large black circle resembling slate, surrounded by black grit. For *Thyestes* there was a knife planted in the ground and a long white table. The simplicity of the set contrasted with the wide variety of costumes ranging from rags to Hollywood get-up. As in the London production, understatement seems to have been the keynote, for as Olivier Schmitt observed: 'the actors are directed without concession to the laws of the genre: neither declaimed nor sung, the text is given a rhythm, a pronunciation of today. Sometimes, the poetry seems to lose its intensity this way, but this decision more often creates an effective feeling of intimacy.' On this occasion, it seems, *Thyestes* was performed not in the traditional French tragic manner, but in a more everyday fashion. Nevertheless, the production was a critical and popular success.

Indeed, so successful was it that Dupont's translation of *Thyestes* was performed in Paris again in December 1999 at the Théâtre de Gennevilliers under the direction of Sylvain Maurice. Michel Cournot's review (*Le Monde*), though consisting largely of a discussion of the finer points of Dupont's translation, something almost unimaginable in the English-speaking world, concluded: 'you will find no pleasure this week in any theatre as lively as a performance of *Thyestes*, Seneca's tragedy, staged directly, nakedly by Sylvain Maurice, in the superb lighting of Philippe Lacombe, spoken by well-built and hard-working actors, and translated by a genuine and fine writer, Florence Dupont. Go, you will leave the theatre utterly stunned by beauty.'[74]

3

Themes and Issues

The finest tragedies are composed concerning a few houses, like those concerning Alcmaeon and Oedipus and Orestes and Meleager and Thyestes ...

Aristotle *Poetics* 1453a19-21

When we examine the plays of Seneca, the actual horrors are not so heinous or so many as supposed. The most unpleasantly sanguinary is the *Thyestes*, a subject which, so far as I know, was not attempted by a Greek dramatist.

T.S. Eliot, 'Seneca in Elizabethan Translation', p. 80[1]

Introduction

Since the revival of interest in Senecan tragedy which began in the latter part of the twentieth century, *Thyestes* has been the play which has attracted most attention and highest praise.[2] And yet not so long ago it was the most despised. Eliot's claim that no Greek had written on such a subject seems intended to suggest that fifth-century Athenian concern for good taste and decorum had prevented their dramatists from exploiting this gruesome myth.[3] Eliot was of course mistaken, for Sophocles, Euripides and others had treated the myth relating to Thyestes.[4] However, their plays on this subject have not survived. The play is, as Eliot says, 'unpleasantly sanguinary', but readers familiar with Suetonius' lives of the Julio-Claudian emperors and with Tacitus' *Annals* will find it no more so than the period in which it was written.

37

Act 1

Thyestes has a structure unusual in ancient tragedy, for it begins with a dialogue between two characters, the ghost of Tantalus and a Fury, neither of whom will reappear in the play.[5] Employment of such characters in the prologue inevitably raises the question of the relationship between Act 1 and the rest of the drama.

The scene is set before the palace at Argos. Before us are Tantalus and an unnamed Fury.[6] It is Tantalus who delivers the opening speech. He is, of course, ancestor to the Argive royal house. Tantalus was also a son of Jupiter, famed chiefly for the killing and cooking of his son, Pelops, in order to serve his flesh to the gods. The event is described in the first choral ode (144-8):

exceptus gladio paruulus impio
dum currit patrium natus ad osculum,
immatura focis uictima concidit
diuisusque tua est, Tantale, dextera,
mensas ut strueres hospitibus deis.

Welcomed by the impious sword, the little son, while he runs to his father's kiss, falls an unripe victim on the altar and is shared out, Tantalus, by your hand, to build a feast for god guests.

For this crime Tantalus' punishment in the underworld was to be tempted by food and drink eternally and eternally to be denied satisfaction. This is alluded to at several points in Act 1 (2, 4-6, 68f., 105f.) and is described in detail in Ode 1 (152-68):

stat lassus uacuo gutture Tantalus:
impendet capiti plurima noxio
Phineis auibus praeda fugacior;
hinc illinc grauidis frondibus incubat
et curuata suis fetibus ac tremens
alludit patulis arbor hiatibus.
haec, quamuis auidus nec patiens morae,
deceptus totiens tangere neglegit
obliquatque oculos oraque comprimit
inclusisque famem dentibus alligat.
sed tunc diuitias omne nemus suas

demittit propius pomaque desuper
insultant foliis mitia languidis
accenduntque famem quae iubet irritas
exercere manus – has ubi protulit
et falli libuit, totus in arduum
autumnus rapitur siluaque mobilis.

Weary Tantalus stands empty-mouthed: over his guilty head hangs abundant prey more fleeting than Phineus' birds. On either side, with pregnant leaves there hangs a tree, bent and trembling with its own offspring, and it mocks his gaping jaws. Though greedy and impatient of delay, so often deceived, he neglects to touch these things, turns his eyes aside, checks his mouth and binds his hunger with fenced teeth. But then the whole grove lowers its wealth nearer, and from above soft apples with languid leaves jump about and ignite hunger, which orders him to move his hands in vain – when he has stretched them forth and enjoyed being cheated, all autumn is snatched aloft and the shifting wood.

Because of his permanently unsatisfied craving, Tantalus is an appropriate emblem for the concept of Lust (*libido*, 46). The fact that he is a child-killer also makes him a fitting ancestor for Atreus.

The primary function of the opening scene is to announce major themes and motifs which are to be explored and developed in the rest of the play. The most prominent of these are hunger and thirst. This is of course appropriate, given the character of Atreus' crime and Thyestes' consumption of his own flesh and blood. Tantalus alludes to his hunger in line 2 and then describes his punishment (4-6):

peius inuentum est siti
arente in undis aliquid et peius fame
hiante semper?

Has something worse been found than burning thirst in water and worse than ever-gaping hunger?

Tantalus also refers to the torments endured by Sisyphus and Ixion, but it is the punishment of Tityus, a giant whose innards are daily devoured by a monstrous bird, which is described most fully (9-12):

> aut poena Tityi qui specu uasto patens
> uulneribus atras pascit effossis aues
> et nocte reparans quicquid amisit die
> plenum recenti pabulum monstro iacet?

> Or the punishment of Tityus who spread open with vast cavern, feeds black birds with excavated wounds and, by night restoring all that he has lost by day, lies full fodder for the fresh monster.

Like Pelops, like the children of Thyestes, Tityus is a being primarily viewed as food.

In the speech of the Fury too the motif of eating is prominent. At line 56 she alludes to 'a Thracian crime', a reference to Ovid's story of Procne,[7] the woman who served up her son, Itys, to Tereus, her husband, in revenge for his rape of her sister, Philomela. At 59-63 the Fury pictures the feast to come. And when Tantalus yields to the Fury's command, his change of heart is represented as an arousal of hunger and thirst (97-9):

> quid famem infixam intimis
> agitas medullis? flagrat incensum siti
> cor et perustis flamma uisceribus micat.

> Why stir up the hunger fixed in my innermost marrow? My heart blazes burning with thirst and flame flashes within my charred guts.

Tantalus' characteristic lust for food now manifests itself as lust for blood.

This is not the only motif that is introduced at this stage. The image of flame is important, for it too is associated with passion, the metaphorical fire in Tantalus' heart foreshadowing the actual fire which cooks the children of Thyestes. And associated with fire are the motifs of dryness and heat. Unrequited lust is associated with dryness (107-14):

cernis ut fontis liquor
introrsus actus linquat, ut ripae uacent
uentusque raras igneus nubes ferat?
pallescit omnis arbor ac nudus stetit
fugiente pomo ramus et qui fluctibus
illinc propinquis Isthmos atque illinc fremit,
uicina gracili diuidens terra uada,
longe remotos latus exaudit sonos.

Do you see how the liquid, driven back, abandons the springs, how river banks are empty, how fiery wind carries off the sparse clouds? Every tree turns pale and every branch stands naked, fruit fled, and the Isthmus, which rages with neighbouring waves on either side, dividing nearby waters with slender land, is now broad and hears far-distant sounds.

The passage of Tantalus through our world has the same effect as his presence in the underworld: desiccation.

If unrequited lust is associated with dryness, then lust satisfied is associated with moisture. Note the Fury's description of the coming feast (65f.):

ieiunia exple, mixtus in Bacchum cruor
spectante te potetur ...

Fill your hunger, let gore mingled into Bacchus be drunk while you look on.

Note too her way of referring to the Trojan war: *effusus omnis irriget terras cruor* ('let flowing gore soak every land', 44). This contrast between dryness and moisture becomes particularly significant in Acts 4 and 5.

A further significant motif introduced at this point is darkness and the flight of the sun. At 48ff. the Fury declares (48-51):

non sit a uestris malis
immune caelum. cur micant stellae polo
flammaeque seruant debitum mundo decus?
nox alta fiat, excidat caelo dies.

Let not the sky be exempt from your evils. Why do stars flash in the sky and flames preserve the beauty owed the firmament?

Her very last words draw attention to the same idea (120f.):

en ipse Titan dubitat an iubeat sequi
cogatque habenis ire periturum diem.

Behold, Titan himself hesitates whether he should order to proceed or restrain with reins a day that is doomed to die.

This idea that the sun was so appalled by Atreus' crimes that it turned backwards in its course is a normal part of the myth.[8] And in fact much of this play takes place in darkness (776-1112).

Also important in Act 1 is the concept of heredity. Tantalus is an appropriate person to deliver the prologue, not only because of the nature of his crime and punishment, but also because of his genetic relationship with the play's principal participants, Atreus, Thyestes and Thyestes' children. Throughout this play Seneca stresses the fact that Atreus' crime has both precedents and successors within the history of the house. Atreus is not the family's only child-killer: Tantalus is his grandfather and Agamemnon, who sacrificed his daughter for the sake of Trojan war, is his son. Thus Tantalus complains that he is being shown his house 'again' (*iterum*, 4), suspects that his family is about to surpass his own misdeeds (*uincat*, 19) and is aware of the guilty nature of his kindred: 'Never, while Pelops' house stands, will Minos be idle' (22f.). In similar vein, the Fury prays that crime infect the family: 'may parents' madness last and go down to their descendants' (28f.) and that each generation will be worse than the last: 'may children perish badly, however let them be born worse' (41f.). Indeed, in the Fury's view, the house is locked into a cycle of crime: *alterna uice* ('by successive alternation', 25), a view that is shared by the Argive citizens who constitute the play's Chorus. Thus in Ode 1 they hope that 'successive alternations of crime might not return' (*alternae scelerum ne redeant uices*, 133), while in Ode 2 they ask what frenzy causes such bloody alternations (*alternis dare sanguinem*, 340).[9] But heredity is not only a determining force in this play. It is also an obsession. Because of Thyestes' adulterous relationship with his wife, Atreus doubts the paternity of his sons (240, 312-33). Only when triumphant vengeance is achieved is Atreus convinced that Agamemnon and Menelaus are truly his (1098f.).

But the first act of the drama does more than announce some of the major themes and ideas of *Thyestes*: it also foreshadows one of the play's major events, in particular, the conversion of Thyestes.[10] It is important to note that the first Act of *Thyestes* does not simply present a dialogue. Tantalus' opening words tell us that he has been dragged on stage against his will, while the Fury's first attempt to arouse him to action results in the ghost's revulsion and his attempt to flee (67). Despite her orders (83-6), Tantalus attempts to block the Fury's entry into the house: *stabo et arcebo scelus* ('I will stand and keep out crime' 95).[11] At line 96 we learn that the Fury holds a whip and it seems clear that when the Fury says *hunc, hunc furorem* ('this, this frenzy', 101) and *sic, sic* ('so, so', 102) she is actually lashing the ghost of Tantalus.[12] The ghost then enters the house and is dismissed after the Fury utters the words *actum est abunde* ('it is amply done', 105). The stage action, the dragging of the ghost onstage, his attempt to flee, his blocking of the entrance into the house and his scourging, underline a point which should be clear from Tantalus' own words: the ghost is a reluctant polluter of his house. He resists the Fury's commands and, initially at least, has to be compelled to obey. In the end, however, Tantalus yields to his instincts (97-100) and infects the house. As we shall see, Thyestes also professes reluctance, but he too is overcome by innate disposition.

Thyestes

Despite the play's title, Thyestes is not the primary focus of interest in this play; he is for the most part an unknowing and unwilling victim. But this is not how Atreus sees him. Atreus is convinced that his brother is exactly like himself, that he has the same lust for power and the same lack of moral scruple. Nothing that happens in the play leads Atreus to alter that judgement. In his first speech, the speech which opens Act 2, Atreus declares (193-5):

> aliquod audendum est nefas
> atrox, cruentum, tale quod frater meus
> suum esse mallet ...

> Some crime must be dared, dreadful, bloody, such as my brother would prefer were his.

Atreus views Thyestes as possessing the same criminality that he does. He also, claims Atreus, possesses the same desire for power (288f.):

> non poterat capi,
> nisi capere uellet. regna nunc sperat mea ...

> He could not be captured, unless he wished to capture. Now he hopes for my kingdom.

In Act 5 as he gazes upon the drunken Thyestes devouring his own sons Atreus says (917f.):

> mixtum suorum sanguinem genitor bibat:
> meum bibisset.

> Let the father drink the mingled blood of his own children. He would have drunk mine.

What grounds does Atreus have for such a view? Primarily, as we learn from Act 2, Thyestes' past behaviour. He was responsible for seducing Atreus' wife, Aerope, and for robbing Atreus of the throne (220-4). And what is more, Thyestes acknowledges his guilt (513f.).

How then does Seneca present Thyestes? He first comes on stage at the beginning of Act 3. Thyestes does not impress us as the kind of man that Atreus claims him to be. He is shabbily dressed and proclaims the value of the life of poverty, the life of philosophic virtue (446-54).

> mihi crede, falsis magna nominibus placent,
> frustra timentur dura. dum excelsus steti,
> numquam pauere destiti atque ipsum mei
> ferrum timere lateris. o quantum bonum est
> obstare nulli, capere securas dapes
> humi iacentem. scelera non intrant casas,
> tutusque mensa capitur angusta cibus;
> uenenum in auro bibitur, – expertus loquor:
> malam bonae praeferre fortunam licet.

> Believe me, greatness pleases with false titles, hardship is feared in vain. While I stood on high, I never ceased to tremble and to fear the very sword upon my side. O how good it is to be in no one's way, to take feast untroubled lying on the ground. Crimes do not enter huts, and food is taken safely from a narrow table; poison is drunk in gold, – I speak with experience: it is possible to prefer bad fortune to good.

Thyestes' professed values are precisely the opposite of those of Atreus. In fact his statements here have much in common with the ode on kingship which precedes Act 3 (336-403). In specifically Stoic terms the Chorus-members also denounce wealth and ambition, associating true kingship with absence of fear and desire and with valuing the peace and security of the obscure life. Consequently some readers accept that Thyestes is an actual or trainee Stoic sage.[13] But if we accept that Thyestes is some kind of Stoic sage and if we take his profession of virtue at face value, then it is puzzling that by the end of Act 3 he has accepted Atreus' offer to share the rule of Argos. At line 540 Thyestes is still holding fast ('my firm resolve is to reject kingship'). At line 542 he gives in: 'I accept'. Why?

To answer this question we need to consider the last phase of Act 3. In his speech Atreus offers Thyestes the crown of Argos. The crown is held suspended between the two brothers. After Thyestes' refusal the following stichomythia takes place (534-42):

45

Atreus:	recipit hoc regnum duos.
Thyestes:	meum esse credo quidquid est, frater, tuum.
Atreus:	quis influentis dona fortunae abnuit?
Thyestes:	expertus est quicumque quam facile effluant.
Atreus:	fratrem potiri gloria ingenti uetas?
Thyestes:	tua iam peracta gloria est, restat mea:
	respuere certum est regna consilium mihi.
Atreus:	meam relinquam, nisi tuam partem accipis.
Thyestes:	accipio: regni nomen impositi feram.

Atreus:	This kingdom is big enough for two.
Thyestes:	Whatever is yours, brother, I believe is mine.
Atreus:	Who refuses in-flowing fortune's gifts?
Thyestes:	Whoever has experienced how easily they flow out.
Atreus:	Do you forbid a brother to gain great glory?
Thyestes:	Your glory is now complete: mine remains:
	my firm resolve is to reject kingship.
Atreus:	I will abandon my share, unless you accept yours.
Thyestes:	I accept: I will bear the name of kingship imposed
	upon me.

What is remarkable about Atreus' arguments is how unpersuasive they are.[14] Indeed they have already been put to Thyestes by his son, Tantalus,[15] and already been rejected. Tantalus has already asked why Thyestes should refuse the happiness that is offered him (430f.). Then Thyestes expressed his fear of Atreus' offer (435). Thyestes has already uttered the political truism that one kingdom cannot have two kings at once (444).[16] Now he accepts Atreus' assertion of the opposite principle as true (534). Given the speed of Thyestes' acquiescence, it is difficult to accept his sincerity when Thyestes professes indifference to wealth and power.

Indeed, if we re-examine what Thyestes says, we can see that he is not as indifferent as he makes himself out to be. His very first words are *optata patriae tecta et Argolicas opes* ('longed-for home of my fatherland and Argive wealth', 404), with the implication that 'longed-for' applies as much to 'wealth' as it does to 'home'.[17] He also recalls his former glories won in his father's chariot (409f.), an ominous remark if we recall that his father Pelops won the kingdom through treachery in a chariot race

3. Themes and Issues

(660f.). He also conjures up a picture of himself being met by
crowds of Argive citizens (411), not the kind of imagining we
expect from a man who truly does prefer obscurity. Nor is
Thyestes' homily entirely convincing (446-70). His account of
the dangers inherent in the life of wealth and power is colourful
enough, but his stated preference for poverty is feebly put:
expertus loquor: | malam bonae praeferre fortunam licet ('I
speak with experience: it is possible to prefer bad fortune to
good', 453f.). 'It is possible to' is less effective than saying 'I
prefer bad fortune to good'. But even so, Thyestes does not
express the idea well. The true sage should argue that poverty,
a condition which most consider bad, is actually indifferent or
even good. The language in which Thyestes states his argument
makes it clear that he still equates poverty with bad fortune.
Moreover, he follows this feebly-stated preference for poverty
with a vivid description of the life he has renounced, a life of
ivory-decked ceilings, bodyguards, fishing fleets, exotic foods,
divine honours, rooftop gardens, heated swimming-pools and
endless drinking. But most revealing of all is the conclusion to
this speech: *immane regnum est posse sine regno pati* (470).
Here Thyestes does not say 'Great kingdom is to be content
without the same to live', as Heywood puts it, or 'Kingdom
unlimited, without a kingdom!' in Watling's words. Rather he
says: 'immense kingdom is it to manage without a kingdom'
(470). The choice of 'to manage' (*pati*) is significant, for
Thyestes claims that he can get by without a kingdom, not that
he does not want one.[18]

There is then a discrepancy between Thyestes' professed and
his actual values. At an intellectual level, Thyestes holds values
akin to those prescribed by Stoic philosophy. At a more visceral
level, he holds the same values as the other members of his
family. It is significant that the son who attempts to persuade
Thyestes to accept his brother's offer is called Tantalus.
Moreover, Thyestes yields to his son in terms that recall
precisely the ghost's surrender to the Fury in Act 1. At line 100
Tantalus yields with the word *sequor* ('I follow'). At line 489
Thyestes yields with the words: *ego uos sequor, non duco* ('I

follow you, I do not lead'). The parallelism between the action of Acts 1 and 3 suggests that it is heredity which is responsible for Thyestes' surrender. His professed values are overwhelmed by his inherited nature.[19]

Throughout Act 3 Thyestes' behaviour is remarkably obtuse. He knows his brother's character (412) and yet he trusts him. Where he was concerned for his sons' welfare, now he hands them over, unprompted, as hostages to Atreus (520f.). He has experienced and is thus aware of the perils of kingship and yet his final gesture in Act 3 is to accept a crown.

But other patterns in Thyestes' behaviour suggest that he is not fully in control of his own actions. After realising that return to Argos means meeting Atreus again, Thyestes commands himself to return to the woods. He attempts to do so, declaring that he approaches the palace against his will: *moueo nolentem gradum* ('I move my unwilling step', 420). And these are not merely words, for young Tantalus comments on his father's weird behaviour (421f.). But within a few lines, we find that Thyestes is drawn in the opposite direction, for his sense of fear now impels him away from Atreus' palace (435-7):

nihil timendum uideo, sed timeo tamen.
placet ire, pigris membra sed genibus labant
alioque quam quo nitor abductus feror.

I see nothing fearful, but yet I am afraid. I want to go on, but my limbs totter, my knees weak, I am borne, carried off in a direction other than that in which I strive.

Thyestes now chooses to approach his brother's palace, but finds himself physically unable to do so. In the end of course the father yields to his son ('I follow', 489). But where Thyestes assigns responsibility for his actions to Tantalus, his son, we might assign responsibility to Tantalus, his grandfather.

Although Thyestes does not appear on stage again until Act 5, he is described in the Messenger's speech in Act 4. In Act 3 Atreus described Thyestes' wretched appearance: his unkempt hair, his woeful face and his foul beard (505-7). Previously

Thyestes professed to take pleasure in his hermit's life. Now the Messenger describes his new condition (778-82).

> lancinat gnatos pater
> artusque mandit ore funesto suos;
> nitet fluente madidus unguento comam
> grauisque uino; saepe praeclusae cibum
> tenuere fauces ...

> The father rips his sons apart and gnaws their limbs with deadly mouth; his hair dripping with flowing perfume and heavy with wine, he glistens; often his blocked-up jaws retained the food.

Thyestes' present appearance strikingly contrasts with his previous squalor. But his luxury is here associated with the utmost degradation. Like his ancestor Tantalus, the seduced Thyestes craves fullness and so he does not feast elegantly on his sons' bodies, but rips them apart and gnaws upon their bones, the words *lancinat* and *mandit* suggesting not human but bestial eating. Indeed, he crams their flesh into his mouth until the food sticks in his throat. Note too the association of moisture with the new Thyestes: his hair drips with flowing perfume, he himself is heavy with wine (780f.). Remember too the association between the unsatisfied lust of Tantalus and desiccation. Here lust satisfied is connected with moisture.

In Act 5 we can see Thyestes for ourselves, for Atreus opens the palace doors and Thyestes is revealed drunken and belching (909-11):

> resupinus ipse purpurae atque auro incubat,
> uino grauatum fulciens laeua caput.
> eructat.

> Reclining he lies on purple and gold, propping his head, heavy with wine, on his left hand. He belches.

Thyestes presents a picture of revolting satiety. Note once more the connection between satisfaction and moisture. Note too the couch of purple and gold, colours suggestive of royalty.

Thyestes' craving for power, as well as for food and drink, has now been satisfied.

At line 920 Thyestes begins to sing a joyful song. In his drunken stupor Thyestes reveals his true values. Whereas in Act 3 he spoke of the merits of impoverished exile, now he sings of *comes exilii / tristis egestas* ('gloomy poverty, exile's companion', 923f.). This is precisely the view that Atreus takes of Thyestes' exile. Indeed, Thyestes uses the very words which Atreus used (*egestas tristis*, 303). The maxim that closes Thyestes' first stanza, *magis unde cadas / quam quo refert* ('it matters more whence you fall than whither', 925f.) constitutes a denial of the views which Thyestes expressed so fervently in Act 3 (446-51). All this suggests that Thyestes has been self-deceived, that the philosophical values adopted during his exile were really a pose, merely a rationalisation of his current state of affairs. Thyestes, quite literally, made a virtue out of necessity. The shift to self-congratulation at line 926 further emphasises his self-deception. He speaks of enduring misfortune 'with neck unbent' (930f.). How ironic given Thyestes' present position, for now he reclines full length (909); now his left hand props up his drunken head (910).

But at line 942 Thyestes begins to alter. He becomes aware of overwhelming physical sensations which he cannot control and whose source he does not know. Thyestes begins to describe his own symptoms like a horrified spectator. In this he resembles Tantalus in Act 1 (97-9), Atreus in Acts 2 and 3 (267-70, 496-505) and himself in Act 3 (419-20, 436f.) and in the rest of Act 5 (985f., 999-1001). One effect of this manner of description is, I think, to suggest that characters are truly at the mercy of forces they cannot control. They are possessed against their will. This might of course point to the operation of heredity. But on this occasion at least there is more than this. His sensations are analogous to the signs and portents which precede disasters. Just as Atreus' crime affects the cosmos, so it affects Thyestes. But despite his sensations Thyestes persists in his delusions: he still trusts his brother.

At line 1005 servants enter bearing the heads of Thyestes' children. After this revelation Thyestes responds with an appeal to Earth (1006-21). Thyestes demands a response to Atreus' crime, insists that an abyss open and plunge himself and Atreus to the underworld for punishment with Tantalus. But note how his speech ends (1020f.):

immota Tellus pondus ignauum iaces?
fugere superi.

Earth, do you lie unmoved, a sluggish weight? The gods have fled.

All Thyestes' distraught rhetoric produces is recognition that his appeal has failed. The earth does not respond. And of course Atreus remains unmoved: he calmly invites Thyestes to enjoy, to kiss and to embrace his sons and then taunts him with a joke: 'What remains of your sons – you have; what does not remain – you have' (1030f.).

After Atreus' informs him that he has eaten his sons, Thyestes speaks again (1035-51), acknowledging divine helplessness and his own. Since invoking the gods is pointless, he appeals to his brother to give him a sword so that he can commit suicide. Atreus refuses. Thyestes begins to pound his body, but realises that he cannot destroy himself without violating his sons' tomb. He concludes with a bizarre paradox: *genitor en natos premo / premorque natis* ('Look, a father, I crush my sons and am crushed by my sons', 1050f.). If the speech seems incoherent, it is because, as Thyestes knows (1037), there is no effective reply to Atreus' deed.

After Atreus' description of his cooking of the children, Thyestes makes a third appeal (1068-96), initially to the seas, the gods, and underworld, and then to Jupiter. Again he acknowledges the flight of the gods (1070) and yet he appeals to heaven's ruler. Rhetorically this is the most effective of Thyestes' three speeches, but again it ends with recognition of his own helplessness. Thyestes entertains the notion that for his sons to receive due cremation he himself will have to be burnt and then concludes by hoping that, if the gods have not heard his prayer, darkness should continue.

It is perhaps the failure of the gods or other forces to respond to Thyestes' prayer which makes the world of this play so terrifying. The gods have been revolted by Atreus' deed, but their only response is to flee. They make no attempt to punish him. There is no suggestion that Thyestes will in any way get revenge upon his brother. All he can do in the rapid stichomythia with which the play concludes is to appeal to the gods again. When Thyestes appeals 'by the gods who watch over the pious' (1102), Atreus replies 'What? The gods of marriage?' a reminder of Thyestes' seduction of Aerope. In his last words Thyestes (1110f.) threatens that the gods will take vengeance. But what sort of threat is this when Thyestes has already acknowledged three times that the gods have fled (1021, 1035f., 1070) and recognised the failure of his own prayer to Jupiter? In the presence of Atreus Thyestes is weak and ineffective.

It is notable that Thyestes moves from scepticism about the gods in Act 3, 'and I see my ancestral gods / (if however there are gods)' (406f.), to seeming confidence in their function as guarantors of the moral order, 'May the gods, brother, pay you rewards in return for your great services' (530f.), to desperate hope that they will defend his cause. Thyestes is the only character who makes such a movement.[20] Atreus has no respect for the gods, indeed, as we shall see, he claims equality with them. Young Tantalus does not bother to pray when he is about to be butchered: 'he did not allow prayers to perish in vain' (720f.). The Chorus moves from a position of trust in the gods to complete despair. They begin with an ode on the due punishment for crime, continue with an ode on kingship which places confidence in moral values, follow that with a meditation on the value of *pietas*, only to conclude in their final ode with a description of the collapse of the constellations, an event which symbolises the collapse of the moral order. Only Thyestes places confidence in divine protection of the world's moral ordering and he of all the characters in the drama has least right to do so. It is not only about his own true nature that Thyestes is deluded.

3. Themes and Issues

Atreus

Atreus dominates the action of *Thyestes*. While on stage in Acts 2, 3 and 5 he either cows or manipulates those around him through his mastery of language. In Act 4 he rules by bestial savagery.

For the Greeks and Romans the world has a three-fold structure, heavens, earth and underworld. Each realm is occupied by distinctive creatures: gods, humans, beasts. One reason why Atreus is so powerful a creation is that he defies these neat divisions, for Atreus is all three: human, beast and god.[21]

That Atreus conceives of the crime he is about to commit as a religious rite is clear from his discussion with the Minister in Act 2. He wonders aloud: 'Tell me, how can I best sacrifice (*mactem*) that accursed head?' (244). So far Atreus might be seen as priest. When the killing of the children takes place Atreus is scrupulous in his observation of religious ritual (684-90):

> ornantur arae – quis queat digne eloqui?
> post terga iuuenum nobiles reuocat manus
> et maesta uitta capita purpurea ligat;
> non tura desunt, non sacer Bacchi liquor
> tangensque salsa uictimam culter mola.
> seruatur omnis ordo, ne tantum nefas
> non rite fiat.

The altars are adorned – who could tell this worthily? He pulls back the young men's noble hands behind their backs and binds their sorrowful heads with purple headband; incense is not lacking, not Bacchus' sacred fluid and knife touching the victim with salted meal. All order is preserved, lest so great a crime take place improperly.

Atreus then is the priest. And the Messenger makes this explicit at line 691: *ipse est sacerdos* ('he himself is priest'). But Atreus is not only priest; he is the one to whom the sacrifice is offered (712-14):

53

sic dirus Atreus capita deuota impiae
speculatur irae: quem prius mactet sibi
dubitat, secunda deinde quem caede immolet.

So grim Atreus gazes upon heads doomed to impious wrath. He
hesitates which one first to sacrifice to himself, then which to
immolate in second slaughter.

Atreus is both priest and god. For all his perverse delight in
meticulous observance of proper forms this is no normal sacrifice. Priest and god are one and the same. And of course these
are not sacrificial beasts, but human beings.

When Atreus enters at the beginning of Act 5 he exclaims:
aequalis astris gradior ('I walk equal to the stars', 885). Since
the stars are conventionally regarded as divinities, as in the
preceding Chorus (*turba deorum*, 843), to claim equality with
them is to claim equality with the gods. But Atreus is not
content with implications. Seeing Thyestes feasting drunkenly
on the flesh and blood of his sons gives him so much pleasure,
so satisfies his cravings, that Atreus declares: *o me caelitum
excelsissimum, / regumque regem!* ('O I am most lofty of gods
and king of kings', 911f.).

The corollary of Atreus' claim to divinity is his contempt for
the Olympian gods. In Act 2 he hopes for crime the gods would
fear (265f.). In Act 5 after claiming equality with the stars,
Atreus rejects the Olympians: *dimitto superos* ('I dismiss the
gods', 888). He recognises the significance of the departure of
the gods: he has nothing to fear. He even wishes he could drag
them back to make them see Thyestes' banquet (893-5). He
refers to the palace, the site in which the children have been
butchered and Thyestes is now feasting, as a 'temple' (902).
Since the principal function which most of the play's characters
expect the gods to perform is to guarantee the world's moral
ordering, a function which they conspicuously fail to fulfil, it
follows that Atreus despises all conventional morality.

The principal exponents of morality in this play are the
Chorus (especially in Odes 2 and 3), Thyestes in Act 3 and the
Minister in Act 2. Let us consider the dialogue between Atreus

and his Minister. After Atreus' opening tirade, the Minister draws attention to the claims of morality. Each cliché that the Minister puts forward Atreus is effectively able to rebut. The Minister raises the threat of popular disapproval. Atreus replies that in his kingdom men are compelled to approve their ruler's actions (205-7). The Minister replies that their praise will not be sincere. Atreus replies that it takes greater strength to win feigned approval than sincere (211f.). Atreus openly advocates tyranny. He has no use for conventional virtues, sanctity, piety and trust (217f.). At 249 he dismisses that cardinal Roman virtue, *pietas*: 'Piety, depart!'. Unlike other Senecan heroes and heroines, Atreus does not even experience moral struggle. And of course he goes on to invert, as Boyle points out, 'the kinds of institution which make human civilised life possible: kingship, sacrifice, feast'. [22] In Act 3 through his mock coronation of Thyestes he inverts the institution of kingship. In Act 4 through human sacrifice he perverts the rites of religion. In Act 5 he corrupts the ritual of the feast.

This brings us to the other side of Atreus' character, Atreus as beast. That bestial qualities reside in the house of Tantalus is stated by the Fury (*ferum / pectus* 85f.) and by the Chorus (*feros ... impetus*, 136). This becomes explicit in regard to Thyestes at line 491: *plagis tenetur clausa dispositis fera* ('the beast is held by the traps we set') and is confirmed by his bestial eating (778f.). It becomes explicit in connection with Atreus when he compares himself to a hunting dog (497-503), when he is compared by the Messenger to an Indian tigress (707-11) and an Armenian lion (732-6). Consider the last of these (732-6):

silua iubatus qualis Armenia leo
in caede multa uictor armento incubat
cruore rictus madidus et pulsa fame
non ponit iras: hinc et hinc tauros premens
uitulis minatur dente iam lasso inpiger ...

Just as in an Armenian forest a maned lion, victorious, broods upon the herd in the midst of much slaughter, its jaws drenched with gore and hunger routed, it does not set aside its anger: on this side and that harrying the bulls, it energetically threatens the calves with teeth now weary ....

Although the beast is exhausted and although its hunger is satisfied, its passion drives it on to still more slaughter. Ultimate satisfaction is not attained.

But this raises an important question. Is Atreus condemned like Tantalus to eternal dissatisfaction? Does his lust simply keep on growing and so refuse the possibility of fulfilment? This might be considered punishment. Certainly one of the most notable features of Atreus' character is his ability to whip himself up, to spur himself on. His very first speech is one of self-rebuke, expressing dissatisfaction with the measures he has taken thus far against Thyestes. But when Atreus conceives the plan to serve his own sons to Thyestes he achieves contentment. In fact his words 'well done, amply done' (*bene est, abunde est*, 279) recall the Fury's satisfaction in Tantalus' infection of the house 'it is amply done' (*actum est abunde*, 105). Even here the satisfaction is qualified for Atreus is content 'for the present' (280). As he gazes upon Thyestes' feasting Atreus congratulates himself again in terms which recall previous occasions: 'Well done, amply done. Now that is enough for me' (*bene est, abunde est. iam sat est etiam mihi*, 889). But then he goes on: 'But why is this enough? I will go on' (*sed cur satis est? pergam*, 890). He then watches Thyestes and reveals to him the truth. But again dissatisfaction comes upon him. Atreus recounts in detail the killing of the children and concludes (1065-8):

> omnia haec melius pater
> fecisse potuit; cecidit in cassum dolor:
> scidit ore natos impio, sed nesciens,
> sed nescientes.

The father could have done all this better, pain has proved fruitless: with impious mouth he tore his sons but unknowing, but unknowingly.

It is this speech which prompts Thyestes' third appeal and it is precisely Thyestes' appeal which brings about Atreus' final satisfaction (1096-8):

> nunc meas laudo manus,
> nunc parta uera est palma. perdideram scelus,
> nisi sic doleres.

> Now I praise my handiwork, now I have won the true palm. I had wasted my crime, if you were not in such pain.

So the beast triumphs. He achieves satisfaction.[23] The only character left dissatisfied at the end of the play is Thyestes, who impotently requests revenge from the departed gods.

I would like to turn now to an aspect of Atreus that relates to an important issue of the play: his awareness of the power of heredity. Seneca brings this issue to the fore by actually bringing Tantalus on stage in Act 1. He also makes his characters conscious of their ancestry. Atreus is well aware of his family's history. He uses the examples of Pelops and Tantalus to spur himself to further crime (242f.). And of course the grove in which the killing and cooking of the children takes place is decked with trophies of the house of Tantalus, trophies of their crimes. But the notion of heredity is important in this play not only in relation to Atreus' ancestors but also to his descendants. Since Thyestes' crime had been to seduce Aerope, his wife, Atreus has doubts about the legitimacy of his sons, Agamemnon and Menelaus (240). Setting this suspicion aside momentarily, Atreus decides that they shall convey the news of Atreus' forgiveness to Thyestes (296f.). When the Minister questions this, fearing that their involvement might lead to their corruption, Atreus brushes this aside: *ne mali fiant times? / nascuntur* ('You fear lest they become evil? They are born so', 313f.). Should they then act knowingly or unknowingly? Atreus decides that his sons should be conscious accomplices (327-30):

> prolis incertae fides
> ex hoc petatur scelere: si bella abnuunt

Seneca: Thyestes

Seneca: Thyestes

et gerere nolunt odia, si patruum uocant,
pater est.

Let proof of their uncertain birth be sought from this crime: if
they refuse war and are unwilling to wage hatred, if they call him
uncle, he is their father.

This question arises again at the end of the play. Atreus is now
confident that Agamemnon and Menelaus are truly his own
legitimate sons (1098-102):

Atreus:	liberos nasci mihi
	nunc credo, castis nunc fidem reddi toris.
Thyestes:	quid liberi meruere?
Atreus:	quod fuerant tui.
Thyestes:	natos parenti?
Atreus:	fateor et, quod me iuuat,
	certos.

Atreus: That my children were born to me, I now believe, that
honour and purity are restored to my marriage-bed. Thyestes:
How were the children guilty? Atreus: They were yours.
Thyestes: Sons to their father? Atreus: I admit it and, a cause for
joy, legitimate.

This passage is both highly compressed and instructive about
the obsessions of Atreus and Thyestes. For obvious reasons
Thyestes is interested only in his own sons. Atreus, however,
oscillates between concern with Thyestes' children and his own.
Thus Atreus begins by declaring that his own children are truly
his. All Thyestes can ask is how his sons deserved their fate.
This question Atreus answers: they deserved their fate because
they were yours. Thyestes is now allowed to utter two words
only, though it is not difficult to infer that he is expressing his
shock that Atreus could feed children to their father. Atreus,
however, prevents Thyestes from completing his sentence. His
reply 'I admit it – ' (i.e. I admit feeding you your children), and
'a cause for joy – legitimate' (i.e. I am now convinced that you
are the father of your sons) is highly compressed and not wholly

58

rational, for he seems to infer that the legitimacy of his own sons implies the legitimacy of Thyestes'. Clearly an obsession with legitimacy is central to Atreus' motivation. But why does Atreus now feel assured that his sons are truly his?

First of all, we should note that this is not Atreus' only claim. Indeed it is not even his most extraordinary claim, for Atreus believes that Aerope's adultery has been undone: 'honour and purity are restored to my marriage bed' (1099). The only parallel to this claim in Senecan tragedy is in *Medea*. In that play after the murder of the first child Medea says to Jason (982-4):

> iam iam recepi sceptra germanum patrem,
> spoliumque Colchi pecudis auratae tenent;
> rediere regna, rapta uirginitas redit.

> Now I have regained sceptre, brother, father, and the Colchians hold the spoil of the golden ewe; the kingdom is restored, my raped virginity is restored.

Like Medea, Atreus is a successful revenger. Like Medea, Atreus is so exultant that he believes that his revenge has not only exacted payment for past wrongs (Aerope's adultery, the consequent slur upon his sons' legitimacy) but has actually reversed, undone them. And that is, presumably, the ultimate goal of all revengers.

Atreus is not merely a crazed and brutal revenger. He is also a consummate master of language. It is not only through physical savagery that he is able to exert power over others. Recall his effectiveness in dealing with the Minister's clichés in Act 2. But it is in Act 5, when he is confronting Thyestes, that his mastery is most apparent. The confrontation between the two brothers falls into two parts. Up to the moment when Atreus reveals that Thyestes has devoured his own sons (970-1034) all that Atreus says is heavily laden with dramatic irony. When Atreus speaks of this day as the one which confirms his kingdom (970-2), Thyestes takes him to be speaking of the reconciliation. Atreus of course is referring to the fact that

Thyestes no longer has heirs who can pose a threat to himself and to his sons. When Thyestes calls for his sons, Atreus replies, 'Consider them in their father's embrace' (976). Thyestes understands him to mean: 'I will bring them along shortly'. We know that they are 'in his embrace' in a quite different sense. Atreus clearly enjoys this game, for he prolongs his speech with a series of ghastly ambiguities. He concludes brilliantly with 'this heirloom cup filled with Bacchus' (982f.). The cup is an heirloom because it belongs to the family, but it is also an heirloom cup since it contains the blood of Thyestes' heirs. At 1005 Atreus reveals the heads and other remaining parts of the children. From this point on Atreus' irony is now mingled with mocking cruelty. He delights in torturing Thyestes, but is still able to play with ambiguities. After the revelation that Thyestes has eaten the children Atreus abandons irony for sadistic pleasure and that sadism is reflected in his language. Thyestes concludes his second appeal with the words: *genitor en natos premo / premorque natis: – sceleris est aliquis modus?* ('Look, a father, I crush my sons and am crushed by my sons. Does crime have some measure'? 1050f.). Thyestes' concluding remark is particularly inept, the words perhaps of someone whose situation is unsayable: if crime has a proper measure, it is because there is a balance of forces between the pressure exerted by his sons on Thyestes and by Thyestes on his sons. But Atreus takes him to mean, 'does crime have some limit'. (*Modus* means both 'measure' and 'limit'.)[24] This of course he denies. He concludes this outburst with one of his most horrifying plays on words: *scidit ore natos impio, sed nesciens, / sed nescientes* ('with impious mouth he tore his sons but unknowing, but unknowingly', 1067-8). Atreus is not satisfied because Thyestes did not know he was devouring his children and because they did not know they were being devoured.

In the final debate with Thyestes Atreus vanquishes his brother utterly. Atreus is ready with his response before Thyestes can complete a question. When Thyestes appeals to the gods Atreus points to Thyestes' own guilty past with the words: *quid coniugales?* ('The gods of marriage?', 1103). Finally when Thyestes entrusts Atreus' punishment to the gods, a futile gesture, Atreus crushingly replies: *te puniendum liberis trado tuis* ('You I entrust for punishment to your children', 1112). Atreus is master in word and deed.

The Chorus

The choral odes of *Thyestes* are as impressive and as carefully integrated with the action as any in ancient tragedy.[25] That all four odes are sung by Argive citizens is not difficult to infer, for this is a Chorus whose concern for the city's welfare is patent. Their first words, an appeal to the gods, underline their concern and their love for their country (122-4).

This is also a Chorus which treasures traditional moral values. The very fact that in the first ode they pray to the gods implies confidence in divine support for the moral order. And in particular they pray for an end to the cycle of violence afflicting the house of Tantalus (132-5):

> aduertat placidum numen et arceat,
> alternae scelerum ne redeant uices
> nec succedat auo deterior nepos
> et maior placeat culpa minoribus.

> May [some divinity] turn kindly godhead here and prevent successive alternations of crime from returning and worse grandson from succeeding grandfather and greater guilt from pleasing their descendants.

Here they pray in general terms. At 136-51 the Chorus-members make specific prayers concerning the house of Tantalus in morally-charged language. Tantalus' offspring they view as 'impious' (*impia*), claiming that there has been enough 'sin' (*peccatum*). They allude to Pelops' 'betrayal' (*proditus*) of the 'deceitful' charioteer (*deceptor*) Myrtilus and describe Tantalus' crime, declaring his punishment deserved (*nec poena decentior*, 150f.).

But if the Chorus-members endorse traditional moral values,

the close relationship between the opening stanza of Ode 1 and the ending of the first Act also suggests that this is a Chorus which is deluded about the circumstances in which they find themselves. At 124f. they refer to the isthmus of Corinth. This can only remind us of the Fury's description of the present state of the isthmus (112-14). And if Tantalus' presence has stripped Cithaeron of its snows (117f.), then Taygetus is not likely to be covered by its 'far-seen snows' (126). Alpheus may normally be a 'clear, cool stream' (130), but it is so no longer (116f.). Moreover, the orderly succession of seasons (126-9) that the Chorus envisages has already been shattered by the unnatural effects of Tantalus' intrusion into the world. For the attentive spectator or reader the Chorus reveals itself not only as moral but ignorant.

But it is in the prayer's conclusion that the Chorus proves most deluded (136f.):

> tandem lassa feros exuat impetus
> sicci progenies impia Tantali.

> At length may the impious offspring of dry Tantalus wearily cast off their bestial impulses.

That such a prayer has no hope of fulfilment has already been demonstrated in Act 1: Tantalus has infected his descendants and we, the audience, know that his sin will be repeated on a grander scale. The Chorus's prayer that such a recurrence of crime should be forbidden will be no more effective than Tantalus' attempt to prevent the crime. Indeed the words they choose *alternae scelerum ... uices* ('successive alternations of crime', 133) are clearly intended to recall the words of the Fury's command: *et alterna uice / stringatur ensis* ('let sword be drawn in successive alternation', 25f.). The Chorus's hopes have already been proved vain. Their conclusion is brief: they hope that Tantalus' descendants might change, if only through exhaustion. They hope that they will cast off their 'bestial impulses' (136). But here too their hopes are vain. The Fury has already commanded Tantalus to excite their 'bestial hearts'

3. *Themes and Issues*

(85f.), and she is successful, for, as we have already seen, bestiality is the leading quality of both Atreus and Thyestes. Moreover, the description of Tantalus' literal thirst (174f.), is immediately followed by the entry of Atreus and his metaphorical thirst for blood and vengeance.

If the Chorus displays its moral credentials in Ode 1, in Odes 2 and 3 they reveal their philosophical inclinations. During Act 2 the audience has been privy to a king's reflections on the nature of power; Ode 2 is concerned with the nature of kingship. Act 3 presents an apparent reconciliation; Ode 3 is a meditation on *pietas*, that sense of familial duty which puts an end to quarrels. Thus the Chorus celebrates the values professed by Thyestes and despised by Atreus.

Odes 2 and 3 both begin with reflections on the events of the preceding act (336-8; 546-8):

> tandem regia nobilis,
> antiqui genus Inachi,
> fratrum composuit minas.

At last the royal house, the family of ancient Inachus, has settled the strife of brothers.

> credat hoc quisquam? ferus ille et acer
> nec potens mentis truculentus Atreus
> fratris aspectu stupefactus haesit.

Would anyone believe this? That bestial, that fierce, that man uncontrolled of mind and cruel, Atreus, stood still stunned by the sight of his brother.

In each case the Chorus is deceived. The opening lines of Ode 2 clearly suggest that the Chorus-members have been tricked by the reports of Atreus' desire for reconciliation with Thyestes; the opening lines of Ode 3 establish that the Chorus cannot understand correctly what is taking place before its very eyes, for it was not Atreus who 'stood still', but Thyestes (*haeret*, 419).

Ode 2 continues with a generalised rebuke addressed to

those with a lust for power, but one with particular pertinence
to Atreus and Thyestes (339-41):

> quis uos exagitat furor
> alternis dare sanguinem
> et sceptrum scelere aggredi?

> What frenzy drives you to shed blood successively and to assault
> the sceptre by crime?

This brief question recalls key words and phrases. Here the
Chorus stresses: the notion of reciprocity (*alternis*, 340)
recalling their earlier prayer and the Fury's command (25); the
idea of rage reminding us of the *furor* with which the Fury
infects the house (27, 101), of the *furor* which fills the heart of
Atreus (253) and of Thyestes' alleged 'rage for power' (302); the
concept of crime (*scelus*) recalling the delight taken in the repe-
tition of this word by both the Fury and Atreus. But what is
most significant about the Chorus's words is that they constitute a question, a question that is not so much a plea for
information as a statement of incomprehension. It is ironic
therefore that they accuse those who lust for power of ignorance of the nature of kingship: 'you do not know' (*nescitis*,
342). But, as we have already seen, the first three lines of Ode
2 establish the Chorus-members' own ignorance. It is an additional irony that the Chorus's observations on kingship have
been immediately preceded by the debate between Atreus and
his attendant, a debate in which the moralist's position was
simply swept aside.

What then is a king? The Chorus's conception of the king is
both philosophical and paradoxical: philosophical because they
define kingship in terms of the possession of moral properties,[26]
paradoxical because they deny that those things which men
commonly associate with kings are essential to kingship. Their
conception of kingship is explicitly Stoic for they deny that
external trappings define what it is to be a king and assert that
freedom from fear and absence of vice are an intrinsic part of
kingship (*rex est qui posuit metus / et diri mala pectoris* ('a king

is he who has set aside fear and the perverse heart's evils',
348f.). At 350-64 the Chorus returns to defining the king nega-
tively, enumerating the qualities which the king will not
possess: he will not be affected by unbridled ambition, by the
mob's fickle favour, by gold, by abundant harvests, by thunder-
bolts or raging seas or military force. When the Chorus turns to
a more positive definition of the king their language becomes
more neutral (365-8):

> qui tuto positus loco
> infra se uidet omnia
> occurritque suo libens
> fato nec queritur mori.

> Who positioned in a safe place sees all below himself and joyfully
> runs to his fate and does not complain of dying.

With this description the identification of the true king with the
Stoic sage is complete, for self-sufficiency, the ability to look
down upon human affairs with complete detachment, is one of
his leading characteristics.[27]

After arguing that the man of good sense is secure in the
tenure of his kingship (*mens regnum bona possidet,* 380), the
Chorus explains that true kingship requires not military
strength but philosophic self-possession (388-90):

> rex est qui metuet nihil
> rex est qui cupiet nihil:
> hoc regnum sibi quisque dat.

> A king is one who will fear nothing, a king is one who will desire
> nothing: each one gives himself this kingdom.

Again these sentiments are Stoic commonplaces.

But what is the dramatic function of these commonplaces?
How, for example, do they relate to Atreus? Although Atreus is
clearly no ideal king, he does conform in unexpected ways to the
Chorus's prescriptions at 344-9. He is indifferent to the trappings of power: his concern is for power itself, not the

accompanying glitter (211f.). He is indifferent to concerns for life and personal safety, since he rates his own life at nought if he can obtain revenge against his brother (190f.). He is indifferent to the 'mob's fickle favour' (351f.), for he values the judgements of his subjects not at all (205-12). Like the sage who sees all beneath himself (366), he will soon 'walk equal with the stars and above all' (885). Atreus may not as yet meet the criteria laid down at 388-90, absence of fear and desire, but he soon will, for by the end of the play Atreus will fear nothing, his sole source of fear having been removed. When about to kill Thyestes' children he shows no fear, showing the constancy of a Stoic sage (703f.). By the end of the play he will desire nothing, for all his desires will have been fulfilled (888). Stoic thought on the nature of kingship proves so inadequate to deal with these circumstances, that it can be argued, paradoxically perhaps, that Atreus meets the established criteria for being a Stoic sage.

What then of Thyestes? Thyestes of course presents himself in a way that recalls the true Stoic sage, professes to have enjoyed his life of poverty (418f.) and the security it offered (449ff.), to be suspicious of the trappings of wealth (455-70). Hence it is not surprising that details in this ode foreshadow Thyestes' homily in Act 3. When Thyestes is self-consciously philosophical there is a remarkable coincidence between his sentiments and those of the Chorus. Just as the Chorus denies any connection between 'beams gleaming with gold' (347) and true kingship, so Thyestes takes pride in his indifference to such vanities: 'nor does bright ivory shine on my lofty ceiling' (457). Just as they assert that the true king has no need of military force (369-87), so Thyestes claims to be secure without arms: 'but we are not feared, our house is safe without weaponry' (468). As the true king is indifferent to death (368), so Thyestes claims to value death above worldly kingship (442).

But comparison between the sentiments of the Chorus and Thyestes' words before his assertion of adherence to philosophic values (404-11) and his subsequent behaviour reveals his adherence to those values to be superficial. Wealth may not make a king (344), but, as we have seen, in Thyestes' opening speech it is the wealth of Argos that is most prominent in his thinking. A king may be unmoved by the mob's fickle favour (351f.), but Thyestes looks forward to the people's reception (411). The true king knows no fear (388), but Thyestes is now afraid (418f., 435). Even more telling are Thyestes' actions. The Chorus claims that neither clothes of Tyrian colour nor a crown make a king (346), but by the end of Act 3 Thyestes has accepted kingship by putting aside his squalid garments (524) and by accepting a crown (531). Thyestes' actions make plain that he is deceived about the true nature of his values. He truly is 'unknown to himself' (403). By the standards established in Ode 2, Thyestes is shown a fraud.

The Chorus proves equally deluded in Ode 3. The inference that the Chorus-members draw from their understanding of the events of Act 3 illustrates their incomprehension of the world of this play: *nulla uis maior pietate uera est* ('no force is greater than true piety', 549). They contrast lasting quarrels between strangers with temporary strife within families: 'true love will hold those it has held together' (551): an extraordinary statement to make in a tragedy, given that in ancient tragedies it is familial strife which is the most intense.

If the first three odes reveal the Chorus's ignorance, the fourth discloses their horrified despair at their discovery of their world's true nature. Now they sing of cosmic disorder, a subject which has been foreshadowed at several points in the play, by the Fury at 48-50 and 120f., by the Chorus on Ode 3 (*dies ... fugiens*, 614), by the Messenger's report that a falling star appeared in the sky as Atreus began his work (698f.) and by his allusion to the sun's flight (776-8).

Enveloped by darkness, the Chorus begins with a series of questions (789-93):

> quo terrarum superumque parens,
> cuius ad ortus noctis opacae
> decus omne fugit, quo uertis iter
> medioque diem perdis Olympo?
> cur, Phoebe, tuos rapis aspectus?

Where, parent of earth and sky, at whose rising all dark night's
beauty flees, where do you turn your journey and destroy day in
mid-heaven? Why, Phoebus do you snatch away your face?

The threefold questions underline the Chorus's urgency. The
unexplained disappearance of the sun at midday has, not
surprisingly, induced a sense of panic, for nature no longer
follows its normal course. The familiar ordering of the heavens
has been suspended.

Nearly half of Ode 4 is taken up with the Chorus imagining the
collapse of the constellations. The passage is almost forty lines in
length (835-74), for the Chorus seems to aim at completeness.
Why this emphasis on the stars? First, for the Greeks and
Romans the stars are conceived of as gods. Indeed this Chorus
calls them *turba deorum* ('a crowd of gods', 843) and *sacris ...
astris* ('sacred stars', 844). To predict that the stars will collapse is
to foretell the end of divine governance of the universe. Secondly,
the orderly motion of the stars and planets is a symbol of the
world's order, both physical and moral. Related to this is the idea
that the gods defend the world's moral ordering. If the visible
symbol of order collapses, where does that leave morality?
Moreover, it is significant that the Chorus speaks of the world's
order breaking down. The unknown crime which has caused this
disorder is so great that the universe cannot contain it. Instead of
responding and punishing this crime, the universe itself collapses.

And it is in the context of a collapsing universe that the
action of Act 5 takes place. When Atreus enters the stage it is
bathed in darkness. This is the first opportunity we have had of
seeing him since the killing of the children and their being fed
to Thyestes. Atreus' success has proved total and consequently
his exultation knows no bounds. He speaks as follows (885-8):

aequalis astris gradior et cunctos super
altum superbo uertice attingens polum.
nunc decora regni teneo, nunc solium patris.
dimitto superos: summa uotorum attigi.

Equal to the stars I walk and touching the lofty sky with proud head above all. Now I hold kingship's glory, now my father's throne. I dismiss the gods: I have attained the summit of my prayers.

The metaphor of reaching the stars is a common means of suggesting the achievement of success in Roman literature. It connotes apotheosis. We should also recall that Atreus sacrificed Thyestes to himself (*sibi*, 713) and very shortly he will exclaim: *o me caelitum excelsissimum* ('O I am most lofty of gods', 911). But there is more than this. Atreus claims not merely to be equal of the gods but to be as high as the stars. He conceives of this in a very physical fashion: he is higher than every creature, his head touches the heavens. Atreus alone now occupies the space once occupied by stars. Atreus views his accomplishment as the greatest of human achievements. For him the gods are now superfluous: 'I dismiss the gods' (888).

But is Atreus right? Can he 'dismiss the gods'? Has the moral ordering of the world collapsed? If we recall Thyestes' passionate but ineffective pleas and his recognition that the gods have indeed fled, if we recall the absence of divine response and the crushing replies of Atreus, we can only conclude that this time the Chorus is right: the gods have fled and the tyrant remains unpunished.

Thyestes and Stoicism

Since Seneca is the author of moral and political treatises, and since *Thyestes* represents a tyrant in full flight, it is reasonable to ask how the play is related to Senecan thought on the nature of political power. In particular, it is pertinent to examine the relationship between the treatment of kingship in *Thyestes* and in *On Mercy* (*De Clementia*), Seneca's principal contribution to political philosophy. Composed in 55 or 56 and addressed to the youthful Nero,[28] *On Mercy*, written in the Stoic tradition of treatises on kingship,[29] elaborates an ideology for the new emperor.

Seneca outlines his ideal of good kingship as follows:

Compare the one who is concerned for all, who watches over
some things more, others less, nurtures each part of the state
as part of himself, is inclined to greater gentleness, even if
punishment were to his advantage, showing how unwillingly
he turns his hand to harsh remedies, in whose mind there is no
enmity, no savagery, who exercises his power gently and advan-
tageously, longing for his citizens to approve his commands,
seeming to himself amply blessed, if he shares his own good
fortune, affable in speech, easy of access and approach, attrac-
tive in appearance, which most wins the people's favour,
disposed to fair requests, not harsh to unfair ones, he is by the
whole community loved, defended, honoured. People say the
same about him in secret as in public. They long to raise children and childlessness once imposed by public evils is undone;
no one doubts that his children will have cause to thank him
for showing them such an era. This *princeps*, safe through his
own kindness, has no need of guards, has weapons for decora-
tion's sake.

On Mercy 1.13.4f.

How different is Atreus' self-description in Act 2. Where the
ideal king is inclined to mercy and is concerned for his people's
welfare, Atreus labels himself as 'tyrant' (177) and defines
himself as 'angry' (*iratus*, 180).

Even more telling is the ensuing debate between Atreus and
his Minister (204-18), for we find that the Minister consistently
advances positions adopted by Seneca himself in *On Mercy* and
that Atreus, with equal consistency, rejects them. Atreus
concludes his opening monologue with the assertion that the
crime lies ready for someone to seize it (204). At this point his
Minister intervenes, asking if the king fears the popular reaction, for he seems to think that, like the good ruler depicted in
On Mercy, Atreus will long for the citizens to approve his
commands. In fact, Atreus despises the people and their appro-
bation (205-7):

> maximum hoc regni bonum est
> quod facta domini cogitur populus sui
> tam ferre quam laudare.

3. Themes and Issues

This is kingship's greatest good, that the people are forced to
suffer as much as praise their master's deeds.

In the Minister's view this is a recipe for hypocrisy, for the glory
of true support is demonstrated by heartfelt, not merely
spoken, praise. And Seneca adopts the same view in *On Mercy*,
for he claims that the people say the same things about the good
king both in secret and in public.[30] This position Atreus also
rejects (211f.):

> laus uera et humili saepe contingit uiro,
> non nisi potenti falsa. quod nolunt uelint.

> Truthful praise often befalls a lowly man, false only the
> powerful. Let them want what they do not want.

To this the Minister's response is to emphasise the importance
of moral leadership: if the king chooses rightly, the people will
want the same. This too is a Senecan position, for in *On Mercy*
he treats the ruler as the soul of the state, as the bond which
unites the commonwealth (1.3.5-4.1).[31] This view is also denied
by Atreus (214f.):

> ubicumque tantum honesta dominanti licent,
> precario regnatur.

> Wherever only honesty is allowed the master, kingship is uncertain.

To this the Minister replies that without modesty, concern for
law, sanctity, piety and good faith a kingdom is unstable. Again,
these are values whose importance is stressed in *On Mercy*, for
there Seneca emphasises the emperor's subjection and account-
ability to the gods (1.1.2, 1.1.4, 1.7.1), the importance of using
power for the people's benefit (1.3.3), the flourishing of virtue
under the just king (1.19.8), and the need for a restoration of
piety and integrity, modesty and good faith (2.1.4). Atreus'
response is a rejection of moral values as appropriate only to
private life:

sanctitas pietas fides
priuata bona sunt; qua iuuat reges eant. (217f.)

Sanctity, piety, good faith, are private goods; let kings go where
they will.

By contrast, *On Mercy* insists that concern for moral values is
even more important in public than in private life (1.5.2, 1.7.3,
1.8.6).

This section of Act 2 presents a contest between a spokesman
for tyranny and a supporter not only of common decency, but of
specifically Senecan viewpoints. Who then is the winner? The
Minister or the tyrant? In one sense there is no winner, since
Atreus refuses to engage with the Minister's arguments: he
merely dismisses them. On the other hand, Atreus' arguments
do have a paradoxical persuasiveness: it may be conventional to
warn rulers of the dangers posed by flattery, but Atreus is right
to claim that it is the truly powerful monarch who can compel
false praise. Moreover, Atreus' rhetorical skill undoubtedly
surpasses that of his Minister: *quod nolunt uelint* ('let them
want what they do not want') outdoes *nemo non eadem uolet*
('no one will not want the same'). But most instructive are the
Minister's lines at the end of Act 2 (334f.):

haud sum monendus: ista nostro in pectore
timorque, sed magis claudet fides.

I do not need warning: loyalty and fear will seal these words in
our heart, but loyalty more.

As Calder points out,[32] the Minister clearly means the opposite
of what he says: it is fear which guarantees his silence. If so,
this is precisely an example of that false praise which Atreus
desires. Here is a man who is compelled to praise, not merely
endure, his master's deeds, a man who is compelled to say what
he does not mean.[33] Atreus' power, both rhetorical and physical,
overwhelms the advocate of Senecan views. Atreus wins.

Just as the Minister embodies views expounded in *On Mercy*,

3. *Themes and Issues*

so does Atreus' realm, for in his prose treatise Seneca presents the tyrant's kingdom as characterised by fear.

> A cruel kingdom is troubled and black with darkness, and among those who quake and tremble at sudden sound even he, who is the cause of tumult, is not unshaken.
>
> *On Mercy* 1.7.3

Fear is all-pervasive in Atreus' domain: it is part of the Fury's curse (40). Fear afflicts Atreus (283), at least momentarily, his Minister, the Messenger (634), the Chorus (828f., 882) and even the gods (266). But above all it affects Thyestes (418, 435). Indeed it is Thyestes who best understands the connection between fear and power (446-9, 482-6).

Moreover, Atreus embodies cruelty as we find it represented in *On Mercy*. Cruelty, says Seneca, is inhuman: 'to rejoice in blood and wounds and, casting off humanity, to change into forest animal, is bestial madness *(ferina ista rabies)*' *(On Mercy* 1.25.1). That Atreus rejoices in blood and wounds is undeniable. Also noteworthy is the fact that Atreus is explicitly described as *ferus* ('bestial', 546, 721) and that he is likened to wild animals (497-503, 707-11, 732-6). He exemplifies 'bestial madness'. Moreover, his cruelty has reached the furthest limit described in *On Mercy*:

> First of all cruelty exceeds normal, then human bounds, seeks out novel forms of torture, summons up skill for the invention of devices whereby pain can be varied and extended, delights in human suffering; then that perverse sickness of the soul reaches the ultimate madness *(insaniam ... ultimam)*, when cruelty turns to pleasure and enjoys killing a human being.
>
> *On Mercy* 1.25.2

Atreus' craving for vengeance, for inflicting pain upon his brother, is represented as unbounded in Act 2. There we see him state explicitly that death is not punishment, but the end of punishment (246). We see his restless search for new devices for inflicting pain. In Act 4 we hear of the pleasure he derives from

73

killing Thyestes' children and in Act 5 we see the enjoyment he obtains from watching and tormenting his wretched brother.[34]

But in *On Mercy* Seneca goes on to list the consequences of monstrous cruelty (*monstrum*, 1.25.4), the chief of which is the fact that communities rise up and destroy tyrants who lord it over them (1.25.3). That Atreus is such a monstrous tyrant is plain, for both he and the Messenger use the term 'monster' of his misdeeds (254, 632, 703). In the play, however, there is no uprising. The Minister acquiesces through fear, and the citizens of Argos, as represented by the Chorus, cower in impotent terror. Once again, Atreus wins.

What then of the good king? He is of course the antithesis of Atreus. In particular, mercy is his primary virtue and he disdains revenge: 'he understands that it is magnanimous to suffer wrongs when power is supreme and that nothing is more glorious than a *princeps* who, when wronged, does not inflict punishment' (1.20.3). By contrast, Atreus rebukes himself for remaining unavenged (178). Although for the good king virtue is its own reward, one of virtue's consequences is a close association with the gods. Hence Nero is encouraged to reflect that he is especially favoured by the gods, that he is their representative on earth (1.1.2) and that he is accountable to them for the condition of the human race (1.1.4). He is told that he should treat his people as he would want the gods to treat him (1.7.1) and that, like the gods, his greatness cannot be diminished (1.8.3). Indeed, the good prince is second only to the gods (1.19.9). Although the true king is not praised in quite such extravagant terms in Ode 2 of *Thyestes*, his position is godlike in some respects, for he sees all beneath himself (366) and lacks both fear and desire (388). But in *Thyestes* it is not the ideal king who achieves apotheosis; it is the tyrant.

Violence

One reason why this play was disliked for so many years is its representation of horrific events, its 'unpleasantly sanguinary' quality. In the second half of the twentieth century critics stood this judgement on its head and saw in the representation of horrific events one of the play's major virtues. Poe, for example argues:

> *Thyestes* has something to say about the enormous satisfaction which Atreus derives from his slaughter, and indirectly about the satisfaction derived by the poet from describing the slaughter or by the reader from reading the description: the play declares that it is the satisfaction of a natural human impulse to violence and ultimately to self-destruction.[35]

That Atreus derives enormous pleasure and satisfaction from indulging his lust for butchery is undeniable. But what of the other half of Poe's proposition, that is, that the poet and his audience also derive satisfaction too from the description? Poe does not go on to establish this part of his case but he is clearly right. The Messenger's speech in Act 4, in my view, is not only revolting but also enthralling and compelling. More objectively, we can say that the Messenger takes great pleasure in his narration of Atreus' deeds. In his opening speech, at the beginning of Act 4, the Messenger displays the same reaction that we would expect of any decent human being: he is appalled by his own news. He is incapable of believing that such deeds could take place in a civilised society. He finds difficulty in composing himself sufficiently to tell of Atreus' deeds and seems to be trying to avoid delivering his message, for he devotes most of lines 641-90 to preliminary description. The Chorus then interrupts briefly at 690 and then again at 716, 719 and 743. But while the Chorus continues to be horrified by the events narrated, the Messenger seems to become more and more enthusiastic for his task. The Chorus asks at 716: 'Which was slaughtered first?' The Messenger replies (717f.):

> primus locus (ne desse pietatem putes)
> auo dicatur: Tantalus prima hostia est.

> The first place (lest you think piety was lacking) is dedicated to his grandfather: Tantalus is the first victim.

At 743 the Chorus exclaims: *O saeuum scelus!* ('O savage crime!'). The Messenger replies: *exhorruistis? hactenus si stat nefas, / pius est.* ('Are you horrified? If the crime stops here, he is pious', 744f.). The Messenger displays the same wit as Atreus. He declares with gleeful irony that in killing young Tantalus first Atreus displays his *pietas*. Moreover, if he had merely killed the children he might well be called *pius*. We should recall Atreus' rejection of the terms of conventional morality. The Messenger comes to share the viewpoint of the murderer. And of course his whole speech is imbued with a marvellous energy and gusto. Here is a case of someone deriving vicarious satisfaction from these gruesome events.

Thyestes as drama

Seneca's *Thyestes* is a meditation on the dehumanising nature of the craving for revenge and the lust for power.

I call *Thyestes* a meditation. How effective is it as drama? Poe defended the play against its critics by arguing that the Aristotelian criteria of plot and character are inappropriate when it comes to Senecan tragedy, because Seneca's concerns lie elsewhere.[36] But this raises a serious problem. If, as we generally accept, plot and character are essential properties of good or effective drama, Senecan tragedy, if it is as Poe describes it, must be either bad drama or something other than drama.

But is Poe's assertion that Seneca shows no concern for these matters correct? Compare *Phaedra*. There is no doubt that in this play character is a matter of central concern, for Seneca provides a powerful representation of Phaedra's emotional state at each point in the play and suggests the sources of her condition.[37] Seneca is as much concerned with exploring psychology in *Phaedra* as Euripides was in *Hippolytus*. Character is equally important in *Thyestes*. Here too the Roman dramatist provides a powerful representation of his protagonist's emotional state and here he is even more explicit about the sources of Atreus' condition than he was in the case of

3. Themes and Issues

Phaedra. And Atreus is considerably more complex a character than those who would assign the play to the category of melodrama would have us believe.[38] Thyestes too is not without complexity. After all he undergoes a transformation from seeming Stoic sage to degraded victim. Seneca manifests as much concern for character as we find in Euripides.

What then of his treatment of plot? To say that in his other major plays, *Phaedra* or *Trojan Women* or *Medea*, Seneca shows no interest in plot is plainly false, for the plots of these plays are neither more nor less complex than the Euripidean versions of the same mythological material. What then of *Thyestes*? Here, it must be admitted, the plot is particularly simple. On the divine level, the Fury urges the ghost of Tantalus to create havoc in the house. He does so. On the human level, Atreus plots the downfall of Thyestes and accomplishes it with ease. The plot of *Thyestes* is less complex than that of other Senecan tragedies.

It is important, however, to observe at this point that *Thyestes* belongs to a category of ancient tragedy that is relatively unfamiliar. This is effectively a two-actor play.[39] Four of the five Acts of *Thyestes* can be performed with only two speaking actors. Act 1 has the Fury and Tantalus, Act 2 has Atreus and the Minister, Act 4 has the Chorus and the Messenger, while Act 5 has only Atreus and Thyestes. The exception is Act 3, where there are three actors, Thyestes, young Tantalus and Atreus. But even here there is no three-way interchange. In the first half of Act 3 there is dialogue between Thyestes and Tantalus and in the second half there is dialogue between Atreus and Thyestes. In this respect *Thyestes* belongs to an archaic category of drama, for we know from Aristotle that Sophocles was the first to introduce the third actor[40] and that three of the extant plays of Aeschylus (*Persians, Suppliant Women, Seven Against Thebes*) require only two actors. Comparison between *Thyestes* and these plays suggests that two-actor form entails simplicity of plot.

But another question arises. Why did Seneca choose this archaic form of drama? The most likely reason is that Seneca wants to emphasise the overwhelming power of Atreus. Complexity of plot implies restrictions imposed upon the central character which he or she must struggle to resolve. In Atreus Seneca wishes to represent an all-powerful tyrant to whom all opposition is as nothing. The manoeuvres to which a Phaedra or an Andromache or even a Medea must resort are not appropriate for Atreus. In Aristotelian terms *Thyestes* may be deficient in plot, but the deficiency is made good by the power of Seneca's representation of Atreus. Indeed the very simplicity is of paramount importance.

Some have considered the character of Atreus overdrawn. But if we consider that the lust of Atreus is exaggerated, we should recall that there was a man at Rome who possessed the power to indulge whatever passion or lust he chose. Emperors like Caligula and Nero indulged in excesses no less shocking than those of Atreus. Consider for example Caligula's megalomania:

> Gaius Caesar, angry with heaven because it drowned out the noise of some clowns, whom he imitated more keenly than watched, and because his revelry was frightened by thunderbolts (surely they were inaccurate), he summoned Jupiter to fight to the death, shouting out that Homeric line: 'lift me or I will lift you'.
>
> Seneca *On Anger* 1.20.8

Consider his cruelty:

> Recently Gaius Caesar whipped and tortured Sextus Papinius, whose father was an ex-consul, and Betilienus Bassus, his quaestor and the son of his procurator, and others, both senators and Roman knights, in one day, and not for the sake of an investigation but for amusement; then he was so impatient of postponing his pleasure, a pleasure so enormous that his cruelty demanded it without postponement, as he was walking on the terrace of his mother's gardens (which separates the colonnade from the river-bank) with some ladies and senators, that he beheaded some of them by lamplight. But what was the hurry?

3. Themes and Issues

> What danger, public or private, did a single night threaten? How trivial it would have been to wait for dawn, to avoid killing the senators of the Roman people while wearing slippers.
>
> Seneca *On Anger* 3.18.3-4

Just as the contemporary Roman world resembles the world of this play, so the play itself is Romanised. *Thyestes'* setting may be ancient Argos, but it nevertheless presents a world whose inhabitants show awareness of lands remote from ancient Greece, of India and China,[41] of Spain and Libya,[42] a world whose borders are threatened by Parthians and Alani.[43] It is a world with Roman household gods, Lares and Penates,[44] with citizens designated by that peculiarly Roman term *Quirites*,[45] with rooftop gardens and heated swimming pools, with rulers who bestow diadems on client kings and a royal palace suspiciously like a more recent imperial dwelling.[46] For an ancient Roman audience the world of this play must have seemed strikingly similar to their own.

4

Reception

Although for us, in the early years of the twenty-first century, *Thyestes* is one of the most potent and most resonant of the ancient tragedies, it has not always been so. For most of the five hundred or so years since its first printing in Ferrara, *Thyestes* has not been highly regarded. And yet at certain periods and in certain places (the second half of the first century in Rome, the fifteenth and sixteenth centuries in England, France and Italy, and more widely in the second half of the twentieth century) *Thyestes* has not only been highly valued but has generated powerful cultural responses. In this chapter I propose to examine a series of works which attempt through reinterpretation either to engage with the issues posed by this remarkable play or to evade them. The task is worthwhile because a study of the reception of *Thyestes* adds not only an important dimension to our understanding of subsequent works, but also to our understanding of *Thyestes* itself.

Thyestes in classical antiquity

There is ample evidence for awareness of Senecan tragedy in antiquity. We find, for example, that Martial parodies *Thyestes* in one of his epigrams, with *nam uigilare leue est, peruigilare graue est* ('for to be awake is easy, to stay awake is difficult', 9.68.10), recalling a remark of Atreus: *leue est miserias ferre, perferre est graue* ('for to suffer wretchedness is easy, to stay suffering is difficult', *Thyestes* 307) (AD 94).[1] A graffito from Pompeii (before AD 79) records *Agamemnon*, line 730,[2] while Quintilian quotes *Medea*, line 453 (9.2.9). But the most substantial evidence of awareness of Senecan tragedy in general, and of *Thyestes* in particular, comes from other works of literature, most notably *Octavia*, a play once attributed to Seneca,[3] and Statius' *Thebaid*.

The sole surviving example of a major dramatic genre, the *fabula praetexta* or play in Roman dress, *Octavia* deals with Nero's murder of his wife Octavia and marriage to Poppaea. Although the play shows marked differences from those of Seneca,[4] the author clearly knew the Senecan corpus well, for he rewrites familiar scenes, with the opening speeches of Octavia and the Nurse being reminiscent of the prologue of *Trojan Women* and Seneca's speech in Act 2 resembling Hippolytus' speech on the succession of ages in *Phaedra*.[5]

However, it is *Thyestes* which is *Octavia*'s most important intertext, for the unknown author clearly interpreted Seneca's play as reflecting the philosopher-tragedian's experience of Nero's tyranny. Act 2 begins with the entry of Seneca himself reflecting, like Thyestes in Act 3, upon the contrast between the exile's life and the life of power.

> Why, unbridled Fortune, flattering me with deceptive looks, did you raise me high when I was contented with my lot, so that welcome in lofty citadel I would fall more heavily and gaze upon so many terrors? I was better off hiding distant from envy's evils, far off among rocks of Corsica's sea, where my spirit free and under its own control always had time for cultivating my studies.
>
> *Octavia* 377-84

Act 3 of *Thyestes* presents a man in the act of returning from exile, a man professing philosophic values, who claims to understand the value of poverty and to fear the life of power, while Act 2 of *Octavia* presents a man, Seneca, who has already returned from exile and is now declining in power; a philosopher, who looking back prefers the freedom bestowed by Corsican exile to the fear entailed by Roman politics.

After reflecting on the pleasure of scientific study, Seneca reflects upon the world's end in terms recalling *Thyestes'* fourth choral ode:

If this (heaven) grows old, destined to fall once more into blind
chaos, the last day is at hand for the world, to crush an impious
race through heaven's collapse.

Octavia 391-4

But where the Chorus in *Thyestes* is utterly despairing, this
Seneca sees hope of renewal in the world's collapse, for
universal destruction will be followed by a better generation
like that of Saturn's age (394-6).

Seneca now offers an Hippolytus-like account of the succession of ages, concluding with the triumph of crime, impiety,
luxury and greed. As if to confirm the truth of this analysis,
Nero now enters, ordering that the heads of Plautus and Sulla
be brought to him (437f.). At this point *Octavia* gives us a
debate between Seneca and Nero which is plainly modelled
upon that between Atreus and his Minister (204-20). In *Octavia*
the exchange is both longer and more regular than in *Thyestes*.
Although Seneca initiates the debate, he is effectively given the
right of reply. Thus when Nero claims that 'It is easy to be just
when your heart is lacking fear', Seneca responds, 'Mercy is the
great remedy for fear'. And so it goes on. Like the Senecan
Atreus, Nero enunciates the rules for tyranny. On each occasion, however, Seneca counters with a statement of moral
principle. Here is the conclusion to their dispute:

> *Nero*: The mob tramples the powerless. *Seneca*: It crushes what
>   it hates.
> *Nero*: The sword protects a prince. *Seneca*: Better loyalty.
> *Nero*: Caesar should be feared. *Seneca*: But loved more.
> *Nero*: They must fear – *Seneca*: Whatever is forced is burdensome.
> *Nero*: Let them obey my orders. *Seneca*: Give just commands.
> *Nero*: I will decide. *Seneca*: Whatever general agreement
>   approves.
> *Nero*: The drawn sword will create approval. *Seneca*: May this
>   crime be absent.

Octavia 455-61

The Seneca-Nero debate is so strongly reminiscent of that
between Atreus and his Minister in Act 2 that it is appropriate

to read this scene as interpreting a Senecan scene with the names of historical characters replacing those of myth.[6] Where in *Thyestes* the Minister represents the common decency of ordinary human beings, in *Octavia* Seneca embodies the moral point of view. But whereas in *Thyestes* each injunction towards morality that the Minister can produce is superbly capped by Atreus, in *Octavia* each tyrannical prescription is countered, though perhaps not overturned, by Seneca. This makes the scene less dramatically effective because neither Nero nor this Seneca is as skilled a rhetorician as Atreus. But perhaps the author is aiming at something different: a less uneven contest between moralist and tyrant.

This brings us to the principal difference between *Thyestes* and *Octavia*. Although in each play the tyrant is victorious, for Thyestes consumes his children and Octavia is led away in chains, *Octavia*'s world is not one of unrelieved despair. First, there is substantial opposition to Nero's treatment of his wife, for the marriage to Poppaea leads to a popular uprising; the people may be defeated but they are not entirely cowed. Secondly, and more importantly, for the knowing reader or spectator the play foreshadows Nero's ultimate destruction through the Nurse's hope that some avenging god might arise (*uindex deus*, 255), a clear reference to Vindex's Gallic rebellion which led to Nero's overthrow (as well as a plain allusion to *Thyestes*, 1110), and through Agrippina's ghost's accurate prediction of Nero's ultimate demise (619-31).

Different in genre, separated in date by a generation, and arising from experience of different dynasties, *Thyestes* and Statius' *Thebaid* (AD 91/2) are nonetheless united in their common concern with the nature of tyranny. Their plots are alike, for both deal with quarrels between brothers, one ruling, one exiled; both end in grisly slaughter.[7] Indeed, *Thebaid* alludes to the Senecan myth at a number of points, to the ancestors of the Mycenaean royal house, Tantalus and Pelops,[8] to the disappearance of the sun and the sudden appearance of the stars,[9] to the deadly banquet,[10] to Atreid cannibalism[11] and to fraternal feuding: 'here too other brothers were joining battle'

(4.308). It has even been argued by John Henderson that *Thebaid* is Senecan tragedy rewritten as epic verse: 'It is in this sense that Statius' *Thebaid* enacted its central role in the representation to itself of its culture, feeding on a marginalised fake-Tragedy, the pseudo-dialogic image-repertoire of Seneca's play-script re-makes, but reinstating Epic form's demand to bespeak Power for social practice'.[12]

Although *Thebaid* is most obviously related to *Phoenician Women* (*Thebais* to the Elizabethans), a play which deals with the same subject matter, the rivalry between Eteocles and Polynices, there are nevertheless close affinities between *Thyestes* and *Thebaid*. Most importantly, Statius' principal tyrant, Eteocles, is closely modelled upon Atreus.

Vessey sees Atreus and Eteocles as stock types: 'Eteocles is, like Atreus, a finished and typical *tyrannus*, crazed with power and scornful of morality'.[13] The proposition that both Atreus and Eteocles are tyrants is not controversial. Atreus rejoices in the name, calls himself 'tyrant' in his opening sentence (177), while the narrator labels Eteocles and his brother 'tyrants' in his proem (1.34).

There are, however, important differences between them. At times we find the Theban king employing moral language and moral arguments. It should be noted, however, that he does so in surprising ways, for his appeals to morality are either hypocritical or perverse. And then there is the fact that fear characterises Eteocles from first to last, from his confrontation with Tydeus in Book 2 until his duel with Polynices in Book 11. Moreover, Eteocles professes concern for the people's welfare, a matter of complete indifference to Atreus. In fact, however, his concern for the Theban people is such that they are only reluctant defenders of their city (4.345-9).

These differences are best accounted for by the fact that we see the two kings in very different circumstances. Atreus' indifference to his citizens' welfare is expressed in private to his attendant. By contrast, Eteocles, as a character in an epic poem, is necessarily a more public figure. We see him dealing with ambassadors and addressing armies. In those circumstances he can hardly express contempt for conventional morality. Secondly, Eteocles depends on others for the securing of his ends and the execution of his will. He cannot defend Thebes alone. Hypocrisy is forced upon the Theban king for much of *Thebaid*. By contrast, Atreus needs to resort to pretence only when dealing with his brother in the second part of Act 3. That which separates Atreus and Eteocles is not their essential nature but their circumstances: Eteocles is Atreus in epic guise.

Thyestes and English Renaissance drama

The generation of dramatists born in the reign of Elizabeth I (1558-1603) is generally reckoned to have been the finest in Britain's theatrical history. This was a generation which had direct access to Latin texts, including Seneca's tragedies, through grammar school education and unprecedented indirect access through the medium of English translation.

The extent and nature of the influence of Senecan upon Elizabethan tragedy is a question both old and vexed. That Senecan revenge tragedy (as exemplified in *Agamemnon*, *Thyestes* and *Medea*) was a primary model for English Renaissance dramatists is evident from the extent to which popular playwrights of the stature of Kyd and Shakespeare quote the Roman tragedian in both Latin and English.[14] My task, however, is not to consider the general issue once again, but to examine the creative exploitation of *Thyestes* by Renaissance dramatists. Since a comprehensive treatment is plainly beyond the scope of this chapter, my intention is to examine in detail a number of works, for which *Thyestes* is a significant intertext, beginning with the first English classical tragedy, *Gorboduc* (1562), continuing with works which exploit *Thyestes* along with other classical texts, Kyd's *The Spanish Tragedy* (1587) and Shakespeare's *Titus Andronicus* (1591), and concluding with two works for which *Thyestes* is the primary intertext, Marston's *Antonio and Mellida* (1599) and *Antonio's Revenge* (1600), and two works which employ classical form and subject matter, Jonson's *Sejanus* (1603) and

Catiline (1611).[15] My aim is to demonstrate that an understanding of Senecan tragedy, especially *Thyestes*, can illuminate
significant aspects of works of some of the most important of
English Renaissance dramatists.

After their first printed edition in Ferrara in 1484,[16] the
tragedies of Seneca were regularly re-edited and reprinted in
the fifteenth and sixteenth centuries, including some twenty-
eight printings of the collected tragedies and six of *Thyestes*
before 1560, the year of the publication of Jasper Heywood's
first English translation of *Thyestes*.[17] The *Thyestes* translation
followed Heywood's successful version of *Trojan Women*
(*Troades*, or, as he called it, *Troas*)[18] which was first published
and apparently reprinted in 1559.[19] Heywood's translations of
Trojan Women and *Thyestes* were then reprinted in Thomas
Newton's collected edition of the tragedies, *Seneca: His Tenne
Tragedies translated into English* (1581).[20] It was the ready
availability of printed Latin texts and of Heywood's translation
which made the reception of *Thyestes* possible.

The effect of Heywood's translation upon subsequent
Elizabethan dramatists is difficult to judge, for his English
version circulated in competition with the original Latin texts
in a world in which major dramatists knew Latin. We can say,
however, that in 1561/2, little over a year after the publication
of Heywood's *Thyestes*, *Gorboduc*, written by Heywood's friends
Thomas Norton and Thomas Sackville,[21] was performed for the
first time at the Christmas Revels of the Inner Temple and
again before Queen Elizabeth at Whitehall on 18 January 1562.
Gorboduc is a landmark play, for it was the first English tragedy
to employ familiar classical devices, the Chorus and five-act
structure, and also the first to be written in blank verse, a
medium more closely approximating Seneca's iambic trimeter
than Heywood's rhyming fourteener.

The extent to which Norton and Sackville were influenced by
Seneca is debated. In the late nineteenth and early twentieth
centuries *Gorboduc* was viewed as overwhelmingly Senecan, the
extreme position being adopted by Schelling who declared that
'*Gorboduc* is pure Seneca'.[22] Such a view was clearly overstated

and self-defeating: only eight plays are pure Seneca and they were composed in Latin in the first century AD. Not surprisingly a reaction set in, with Baker declaring that many so-called Senecan ideas were commonplace and that the five-act form was actually derived from ancient comedy.[23]

The question of five-act form is readily resolved. Baker declares: 'The English play, it is true, has five acts, but several circumstances indicate that this mode of division may, in greater likelihood, have been derived from the classical comedies'.[24] Although it is true that ancient theoreticians recommended a five-act structure,[25] there are no complete plays from the ancient world which exhibit a five-act structure apart from Seneca's. The Roman comic playwrights Plautus and Terence did not divide their plays in this way: the five-act structure had to be imposed upon them by editors. By contrast, leaving aside the apparently incomplete *Phoenician Women*, Seneca's plays employ alternating action and choral odes, with the norm being five acts and four odes. Given that Norton and Sackville employ choral odes as act-dividers and given that Plautus and Terence do not use the Chorus at all, the obvious model for *Gorboduc*'s dramatic structure, including the use of five acts, is Senecan tragedy, not Roman comedy. This is not, however, to assert that *Gorboduc*'s dramatic structure is 'pure Seneca', for the use of the dumb show before the beginning of each act has no classical precedent. Neither is the handling of the Chorus Senecan, for *Gorboduc*'s odes seem to reiterate the moral outlined in the dumb show and to confirm the stated interpretation of the play's action. For example, the dumb show which precedes Act 1 presents six men who fail when they attempt to break a bundle of sticks, but succeed when they snap them individually. After Act 1 and Gorboduc's resolution to divide his realm between his sons, the first Chorus picks up the image of the sticks and then denounces Gorboduc's decision. Where in Seneca the relationship between ode and act is complex, in *Gorboduc* the Chorus seems always to act as the dramatists' mouthpiece.

That Norton and Sackville were acquainted with the corpus

of Senecan tragedy (including the pseudo-Senecan *Octavia*) is apparent from the play's beginning, for Videna's opening speech is reminiscent of the opening of *Octavia*, while Gorboduc's meditation on the destinies suffered by the Trojans and their descendants, of whom he reckons himself one, are plainly modelled on Hecuba's similar reflections in the opening speech of *Trojan Women*, even to the point of calling Priam 'happy'.[26]

It is in the play's concern with the destructiveness of the pursuit of power, the 'lust of kingdom',[27] that its exploitation of *Thyestes* is most apparent. Central to Act 2 is the danger posed by flatterers. The second dumb show presents a king offered two cups of wine:

> And after he had placed himself in a chair of estate prepared for him, there came and kneeled before him a grave and aged gentleman, and offer'd up a cup unto him of wine in a glass, which the king refused. After him comes a brave and lusty young gentleman, and presents the king with a cup of gold filled with poison, which the king accepted, and drinking the same, immediately fell down dead upon the stage.

The second Chorus picks up the image, concluding with the words:

> Lo thus it is, poison in gold to take,
> And wholesome drink in homely cup forsake.

The idea that poison is drunk from a golden cup is foreshadowed by a remark of Thyestes' (452f.):

> tutusque mensa capitur angusta cibus;
> uenenum in auro bibitur – expertus loquor.

> Food is safely taken from a narrow table; poison is drunk from gold – I speak from experience.

Act 2 of *Gorboduc* enacts Thyestes' comment.

Equally important are that Gorboduc, like Thyestes, fails to observe the maxim that kingship is not room enough for two (*non capit regnum duos*, 444), that Ferrex desires punishment in terms reminiscent of Senecan hell, listing Tantalus, Ixion and Tityos,[28] that the third Chorus reverses the moral sentiments of *Thyestes'* choral odes, claiming that 'the lust of kingdom knows no sacred faith' and that Megaera and Tantalus are present in the fourth dumb show, Megaera being the Senecan Fury's name in Renaissance texts. But most important of all is the Atreus-like advice which Hermon gives to Ferrex in Act 2, Scene 1. Having urged Ferrex to invade his brother's territory and listed his practical advantages, Hermon goes on to discount the gods:

> But if the fear of gods, and secret grudge
> Of nature's law, repining at the fact,
> Withhold your courage from so great attempt,
> Know ye, that lust of kingdoms hath no law.
> The gods do bear, and well allow in kings,
> The things that they abhor in rascal routs.
> And then in cruel and unkindly wise
> Command thefts, rapes, murders of innocents,
> The spoil of towns, ruins of mighty realms;
> Think you such princes do suppose themselves
> Subject to laws of kind, and fear of gods?
> Murders and violent thefts in private men
> Are heinous crimes, and full of foul reproach;
> Yet none offence, but deck'd with glorious name
> Of noble conquests, in the hands of kings.
>
> *Gorboduc* 2.1.140-55

Act 2, Scene 1 presents a counselling scene reminiscent of *Thyestes* Act 2. However, whereas in *Thyestes* there is a king who overrides his counsellor's advice, in *Gorboduc* there are two counsellors, one good, one bad, and a king, Ferrex, who foolishly adopts a compromise position. It is Hermon, the wicked mentor, who acts as spokesman for the views of Atreus, urging the king to kill his younger brother. In particular Hermon's argument that the gods tolerate in kings what they abhor in ordinary mortals reflects Atreus' contempt for divine sanctions, while his argument that misdeeds of 'private men / Are heinous crimes' recalls Atreus' argument that moral values are for private life and that kings should go where they please (*sanctitas pietas fides / priuata bona sunt; qua iuuat reges eant*, 217f.).

If Schelling's view that *Gorboduc* is 'pure Seneca' was overstated, so too was Baker's insistence on the exclusive importance of native traditions and denial of Senecan influence. That Norton and Sackville exploited *Thyestes* seems clear enough, but their work also manifests distinctly non-Senecan features, including use of the dumb-show and scenes involving four or more speakers.[29] Equally extreme and equally self-defeating is Baker's insistence that *Gorboduc* is either Senecan or concerned with Elizabethan politics, for that is to ignore the political dimension of Senecan tragedy: 'Senecan' and 'political' are not antithetical terms. Both *Thyestes* and *Gorboduc* are concerned with the nature of monarchy.

It is regularly asserted that Senecan tragedy in general and *Thyestes* in particular are fundamental to the development of revenge tragedy in Elizabethan England. Thus Watson claims that 'the efficient cause for the prevalence of revenge plots in English tragedy is the example of Seneca'. He goes on to observe that 'the revenger is usually a powerless outsider avenging an inflammatory offence to a lover or close kin'.[30] As a description of English revenge plays, Watson's statement is of course accurate. It also happens to be a fair summary of Seneca's *Medea*, a play whose eponymous heroine is excluded from legitimate society, and of his *Agamemnon*, where the principal revengers, Clytemnestra and Aegisthus, are usurpers and murder the rightful king of Argos. It is not, however, accurate as a summary of *Thyestes*, for Atreus is no longer an outsider excluded from access to justice: he is the king. There are, then, important differences between Atreus and the revengers whom I propose to consider: men like Hieronimo, Titus and Antonio.

Kyd and Shakespeare are, needless to say, more sophisticated exploiters of *Thyestes* and other classical texts than Norton and

Sackville. Thomas Kyd's play *The Spanish Tragedy* invokes various works, especially Virgil's *Aeneid* and a number of Senecan tragedies. The experience of Andrea's ghost in the underworld follows closely that of Aeneas as reported in Book 6. There is however, one significant exception, for whereas Aeneas leaves through the ivory gate, the gate through which false dreams exit (6.896), Andrea is sent 'through the gates of horn' (1.1.82), for his is a dream of vengeance which will be fulfilled.[31] But if Andrea's account of the underworld is basically Virgilian, the context in which he delivers it is reminiscent of *Thyestes*, for in both plays we have a prologue in which a ghost (Tantalus/Andrea) and an allegorical figure (Fury/Revenge) speak of revenge. Scene 1 closes with a command:

> Here sit we down to see the mystery,
> And serve for Chorus in this tragedy.
>
> *The Spanish Tragedy* 1.1.90-1

And so the play proceeds with each of the four acts closing with a conversation between Andrea and Revenge serving as Kyd's version of a choral ode.[32] Further, having Andrea and Revenge watch the play's action might well have been prompted by the Fury's command that Tantalus watch the drinking of wine and blood (*spectante te potetur*, 66). As Mercer observes, 'The ghost of Andrea, in *The Spanish Tragedy*, is plainly of Senecan descent.'[33]

However, this is not to suggest that Kyd's play is any sense derivative. Indeed, his handling of the prologue implies otherwise: Andrea does not need the incitement of Revenge to make him crave retaliation and here there is no emphasis on inherited lust for blood, for Andrea is not even related to Hieronimo, the play's revenger. Nor is there vigorous exchange between the two characters. And Kyd's version of a chorus is very different from Seneca's. I am, however, suggesting that *The Spanish Tragedy* is explicitly concerned with issues raised by Senecan drama.

That this is so is confirmed by Kyd's use of quotation. In addition to Virgil, Kyd makes use of Alain of Lille,[34]

Claudian,[35] Lucretius,[36] Ovid,[37] Statius[38] and Tibullus.[39] But it is Seneca who is of prime dramatic significance, for denial of justice for Horatio's death leads Hieronimo to set the Christian prohibition of revenge against the imperative exemplified in Senecan tragedy. Hieronimo enters in Act 3, Scene 13 'with a book in his hand', the book clearly being a volume of Seneca's tragedies, and delivers what is commonly regarded as the play's most important speech. He begins by citing and expounding *Romans* 12.19:[40]

> *Vindicta mihi!*
> Ay, heaven will be revenged of every ill,
> Nor will they suffer murder unrepaid:
> Then stay Hieronimo, attend their will,
> For mortal men may not appoint their time.
>
> *The Spanish Tragedy* 3.13.1-5

At this point Hieronimo reads from Seneca, slightly misquoting Clytemnestra's words at *Agamemnon* 115:

> '*Per scelus semper tutum est sceleribus iter*'
> Strike, and strike home where wrong is offered thee;
> For evils unto ills conductors be,
> And death's the worst of resolution.
> For he that thinks with patience to contend
> To quiet life, his life shall easily end.

In their context Clytemnestra's words (*per scelera semper sceleribus tutum est iter*, 'through crimes always is the safe path for crimes') form part of a self-exhortation to the murder of Agamemnon, since for the adulterous queen the killing of her husband is the only course of action which offers safety. For Hieronimo these words are a reminder that Lorenzo is in a similar position: he may resort to crime to conceal his murder of Horatio ('For evils unto ills conductors be'). To act is preferable to patience, to leaving vengeance to heaven, for that may lead to his own death.[41]

At this point Hieronimo quotes two lines of Andromache from *Trojan Women* (510-12):[42]

Seneca: Thyestes

'*Fata si miseros juvant, habes salutem*';
If destiny thy miseries do ease,
Then thou hast health, and happy shalt thou be;
If destiny deny thee life, Hieronimo,
Yet shalt thou be assured of a tomb;
If neither, yet let this thy comfort be,
Heaven covereth him that hath no burial.
And to conclude, I will revenge his death!

The Spanish Tragedy 3.13.12-20

Andromache's words ('If fate helps the wretched, you have your safety/health; / If fate denies you life, you have your tomb') are addressed to her young son, Astyanax, who is to be hidden in his father's sepulchre for protection against the vengeful Greeks, and are intended as consolation. Hieronimo distorts Andromache's words into an exhortation to revenge.

How is this accomplished? Reflection upon Clytemnestra's words has led Hieronimo to the conclusion that he must act in order to obtain revenge. Now he reflects upon the possible consequences of action. Either he will succeed or he will not. If destiny favours and he is successful, then he will achieve health and happiness. If destiny does not favour him and he loses his life, then at least he will have a tomb. If he wins neither happiness nor tomb, then heaven will provide burial. Thus no matter what the outcome, only one course of action is appropriate. Once again reflection upon a Senecan text prompts the conclusion that Hieronimo's situation demands revenge. The fact that in this case the Latin words do not support Hieronimo's reasoning suggests that here we see not a man reaching a conclusion, but a man appealing to textual authority for a decision already reached.

The next question for Hieronimo is how to achieve revenge. Here the answer is easy for what is required is concealment:

Thus therefore will I rest me in unrest,
Dissembling quiet in unquietness,
Not seeing that I know their villainies;
That my simplicity may make them think
That ignorantly I will let all slip –

4. Reception

For ignorance, I wot, and well they know,
Remedium malorum iners est.

The Spanish Tragedy 3.13.29-35

Hieronimo concludes by adapting words from Seneca's *Oedipus*. When Creon, having returned from Delphi, attempts to conceal what he has learned, Oedipus remarks: *iners malorum remedium ignorantia est* (515, 'ignorance is weak remedy for evil'), meaning that without knowledge he cannot save Thebes. Although *Oedipus*, like *Trojan Women*, is not a revenge tragedy, Hieronimo cannot be said to distort the meaning of Oedipus' remark, for he argues that his enemy's awareness of the truth of this proposition will serve as his protection: feigned ignorance will protect his life.

For Hieronimo the limits of his choices are defined by Christian principle and Senecan example. Beginning as an embodiment of justice, as Knight Marshal of Spain, he is driven insane with grief and becomes a brutal and joyful killer. Having killed Lorenzo, Hieronimo goes on to bite out his own tongue and to knife Don Cyprian and himself. In his savage brutality Hieronimo resembles no one so much as Atreus. It is fitting then that the play closes with the return of Andrea and Revenge to hell and a description of the underworld more reminiscent of the opening speeches of *Agamemnon* and *Thyestes* than of Virgil's *Aeneid*. Unable to obtain justice, Hieronimo rejects Christian principles and is transformed into a Senecan revenger.

Since Howard Baker's *Induction to Tragedy* (1939) it has become conventional to assert that Shakespeare's *Titus Andronicus*[43] shows no signs of Senecan influence and that the poet's sole debt is to Ovid.[44] The truth is that *Titus Andronicus* invokes various classical texts.[45] Horace is quoted and Livy is referred to.[46] Virgil is important,[47] because the quasi-marriage between Dido and Aeneas is presented as a model for both the rape of Lavinia by Chiron and Demetrius[48] and the relationship between Tamora and Aaron.[49] Further, Virgil's account of the Greek sack of Troy in *Aeneid* 2 is crucial, for, as Miola points out, 'the archetypal invasion of the civilised Trojan city by the barbarian Greeks is reenacted on stage as the civilised Roman city is invaded by barbarian Goths'.[50]

Still more important for this play is Ovid, for we find constant allusion to myths which had been given their definitive form in *Metamorphoses* and *Fasti*. Thus we find references to Hecuba,[51] Ajax,[52] Lucretia,[53] the house of Fame,[54] Diana and Actaeon,[55] Pyramus,[56] Orpheus,[57] Io,[58] Astraea[59] and the battle between the Lapiths and Centaurs.[60] But by far the most important Ovidian model is the story of Philomela (*Metamorphoses* 6.424-674), a gruesome myth whose gruesomeness the play surpasses, for where Tereus cuts out Philomela's tongue, Demetrius and Chiron not only cut out Lavinia's tongue but also lop off her hands to prevent her from imitating Philomela, who wove her story and so informed her sister of her fate.[61] As Marcus observes:

> Fair Philomela, why she but lost her tongue,
> And in a tedious sampler sew'd her mind;
> But, lovely niece, that mean is cut from thee.
> A craftier Tereus, cousin, hast thou met,
> And he hath cut those pretty fingers off,
> That could have better sew'd than Philomel.
>
> *Titus Andronicus* 2.3.38-43

That Ovid provides the model for this portion of the play is underlined by the fact that Lavinia uses a copy of the *Metamorphoses* to reveal what has been done to her:

> Titus: Lucius, what book is that she tosseth so?
> Boy: Grandsire, 'tis Ovid's *Metamorphosis*;
>   My mother gave it me.
> Marcus: For love of her that's gone,
>   Perhaps she culled it from among the rest.
> Titus: Soft! see how busily she turns the leaves!
>   *Helps her*
>   What would she find? Lavinia, shall I read?
>   This is the tragic tale of Philomel,
>   And treats of Tereus' treason and his rape –
>   And rape, I fear, was root of thy annoy.
>
> *Titus Andronicus* 4.1.41-9

4. Reception

The importance of Ovid to this play is undeniable.

But Ovid's importance need not diminish Seneca's. If Shakespeare quotes Ovid in Latin, he quotes more Seneca.[62] At the end of Act 1, while plotting the rape of Lavinia, Demetrius paraphrases words of Phaedra: *Per Stygia, per manes vehor* (1.1.635, 'through Stygian [regions], through ghosts I am borne'). In their original context Phaedra's words (*per Styga, per amnes igneos amens sequar*, 'through Styx, through fiery rivers, mad I will follow you', *Phaedra* 1180) are addressed to the dead Hippolytus and suggest that even on the point of death she is unable to control her passion. Demetrius too is overcome by lust. In Demetrius' line Shakespeare rings another change upon Seneca's verbal play, for *amnes* ('rivers') and *amens* ('mad') have now become *manes* ('ghosts') and the active *sequar* ('I will follow') has become the passive *vehor* ('I am carried'), suggesting that Demetrius is even less self-controlled than Phaedra. In Act 4, Scene 1 we find Titus paraphrasing Seneca:

> Magni dominator poli,
> tam lentus audis scelera, tam lentus vides?
>
> *Titus Andronicus* 4.1.81-2

Master of great heaven, / Are you so indifferent when you hear of crimes, so indifferent when you see them?

Once again the quotation comes from *Phaedra*:

> Magne regnator deum,
> tam lentus audis scelera? tam lentus uides?
>
> *Phaedra* 671f.

Great ruler of gods, are you so indifferent when you hear of crimes, so indifferent when you see them?

Here the change is even less, just enough to remove a reference to polytheism. Again the quotation is wholly apposite to its context, for Titus' shock at the crime wrought upon his daughter echoes Hippolytus' horror at Phaedra's proposal of

97

incestuous adultery. Shakespeare clearly knew Seneca's *Phaedra* well.

But what of *Thyestes*? Here the problem has been the similarity between the final part of Ovid's telling of the myth of Philomela and the plot of *Thyestes*. Indeed, Seneca, like Shakespeare, uses Tereus and Philomela as a 'sampler', for Atreus is aware of the precedent of 'the Odrysian house' and the 'Daulian mother' and consciously strives to surpass them (272-6).[63] Even if Shakespeare had exploited only elements common to the two myths, elements like the killing, cooking and devouring of a child or children, we would not be justified in excluding allusion to *Thyestes*. In fact, however, Shakespeare does exploit elements which are found in *Thyestes* and not in *Metamorphoses* 6.

Perhaps the most striking recasting of a motif drawn from *Thyestes* is the radical reshaping of Ode 4 into a scene in which Titus and his kinsmen shoot arrows into the emperor's court as a way of seeking justice (4.3). Astonished that the world has suddenly been plunged into darkness, the fourth Chorus of *Thyestes* predicts the zodiac's collapse (843-74):

> The mass of gods will go heaped into a single cavity: this zodiac, traversed by sacred stars, which cuts the zones in slanting path, turning the long years, falling will see the fallen stars. This Aries, who restores sails to warm Zephyr when spring is not yet kind, will go headlong into the waves, through which he bore trembling Helle. This Taurus, who bears before him the Hyades on shining horn, will drag down Gemini with himself and the arms of curving Cancer.
>
> Herculean Leo, blazing with burning heat, will fall from the sky again, and Virgo will fall to the earth which she abandoned, and the weights of just Libra will drag down with themselves fierce Scorpio. And aged Chiron who holds feathered darts to Haemonian string will lose darts, his string broken. Cold Capricorn, restorer of sluggish winter, will fall and you, whoever you are, will break your urn. With you will depart heaven's furthest stars, Pisces, and the all-overwhelming flood will drown monsters never dipped in sea. And the slippery Snake which

river-like divides the Bears in two and the Lesser Bear,
Cynosura, cold with hard ice, joined to the great Dragon, and the
sluggish guard of his own Wagon, Arctophylax, no longer stable,
will collapse.

This image of collapsing constellations Shakespeare transforms
into action:

Titus:	And, sith there's no justice in earth nor hell,
	We will solicit heaven and move the gods
	To send down Justice for to wreak our wrongs.
	Come, to this gear. You are a good archer, Marcus
	He gives them the arrows.
	'*Ad Jovem*', that's for you: here, '*Ad Apollinem*'.
	'*Ad Martem*', that's for myself;
	Here, boy, 'to Pallas'. Here, 'to Mercury'.
	'To Saturn', Caius – not 'to Saturnine'!
	You were as good to shoot against the wind.
	To it, boy! Marcus, loose when I bid.
	Of my word, I have written to effect:
	There's not a god left unsolicited.
Marcus:	Kinsmen, shoot all your shafts into the court;
	We will afflict the emperor in his pride.
Titus:	Now, masters, draw. *They shoot.*
	O, well said, Lucius,
	Good boy: in Virgo's lap! give it Pallas.
Marcus:	My lord, I aimed a mile beyond the moon:
	Your letter is with Jupiter by this.
Titus:	Ha, ha! Publius, Publius, what hast thou done?
	See, see, thou hast shot off one of Taurus' horns.
Marcus:	This was the sport, my lord: when Publius shot,
	The Bull, being gall'd, gave Aries such a knock
	That down fell both the Ram's horns in the court.

Titus Andronicus 4.3.50-72

The episode presents Titus distributing arrows addressed, as it
were, to the gods or planets[64] and then Titus and Marcus
boasting that they have shot down the constellations. That
Titus and Marcus should associate the failure of divine justice
with falling stars is entirely appropriate, for that is precisely the
image's significance in *Thyestes*.[65] As De Armas observes, 'the

third scene of the fourth act emulates and comments upon the fourth Chorus in *Thyestes*'.[66]

There are more general resemblances between the two plays, for as Miola argues, 'directly or indirectly, *Thyestes* lies behind the action of *Titus Andronicus*, a deep source of its energy and its aesthetic of violence'.[67] Thus in both plays we see the corruption of major cultural institutions: in *Thyestes* Atreus inverts 'the kinds of institution which make human civilised life possible: kingship, sacrifice, feast',[68] while in *Titus Andronicus* 'all the major ceremonies of Elizabethan society that uphold civilization are undone'.[69] In both plays we see a confusion between civilisation and barbarism, between Greek and Scythian in *Thyestes*,[70] between Roman and Goth in *Titus*. Indeed, it seems possible that *Thyestes'* emphasis on the bestiality of human beings (note especially the likening of Atreus to a Ganges tigress, 707ff.) lies behind *Titus'* representation of Rome as 'a wilderness of tigers' (3.1.54). And of course both plays climax in a cannibalistic banquet. The conclusion that in *Titus Andronicus* Shakespeare reworks both *Metamorphoses* 6 and Seneca's *Thyestes* seems inescapable.

In Marston's *Antonio* plays we see a less radical but equally sophisticated engagement with *Thyestes*. If quotation means anything, *Antonio and Mellida* should be one of the most Senecan of Renaissance dramas, for Marston quotes in either Latin or English from *Octavia*,[71] *Phaedra*,[72] *Agamemnon*,[73] *Medea*,[74] *Trojan Women*,[75] *Oedipus*,[76] *Phoenician Women*,[77] *Hercules on Oeta*[78] and, above all, *Thyestes*. In tone and subject matter, however, *Antonio and Mellida* is far removed from Senecan tragedy, for the plot concerns the innocent love of Antonio and Mellida, alternates humorous and serious scenes and includes such comic characters as Castilio and Forobosco, Mazzagente and Galeazzo, Rosaline and Flavia, Cazzo and Dildo and the fatuous Balurdo. The play even has an apparently happy ending. In short, *Antonio and Mellida* is, as Finkelpearl observes, 'a Senecan comedy'.[79]

This might suggest that Marston's allusions to Senecan tragedy are incidental, superficial. However, examination of allusions to *Thyestes* suggests that quotation is Marston's primary means of highlighting interest in significant Senecan issues.

Marston's concern with the nature of power is apparent from the play's first scene. From Antonio's opening soliloquy we learn that he and his father, Andrugio, the duke of Genoa, have just been defeated by Piero, prince of Venice. Cornets then sound to announce Piero's triumphant entry. When warned by Felice of pride's dangers, Piero, quotes words of the victorious Atreus (*Thyestes* 888) and cries out: 'Pish! *Dimitto superos, summa uotorum attigi*' ('I dismiss the gods, I have attained the peak of my desires', 1.1.60).[80] Later in the same scene, having learned that his orders proclaiming a reward for the heads of Andrugio and Antonio have been carried out, Piero exclaims 'Why then *O me caelitum excelsissimum*' ('O I am most lofty of gods', 1.1.78), quoting the words of Atreus when he first sees his sated brother (*Thyestes* 911). Quotation establishes Piero as a tyrant of Atreid aspirations. There are, however, significant differences between Atreus' and Piero's circumstances, for Piero's quotations are spoken in Act 1, while Atreus' words come from Act 5: beginning from so high a summit Piero must surely fall. And Piero seems to fall, for *Antonio and Mellida* closes with a reconciliation between Piero and his enemies, with Piero sparing Andrugio's life and allowing Antonio to marry Mellida. However, this reconciliation, like that between Atreus and Thyestes, proves false, for in the opening scene of *Antonio's Revenge* we see Piero's pride in murder and deception. From Piero's perspective the action of *Antonio and Mellida* looks like *Thyestes* in reverse, for where Atreus moves from fake forgiveness to unqualified victory, we see Piero move from unqualified victory to fake forgiveness.

But Piero is not the only character in Marston's play with Senecan associations, for both Felice and Andrugio express sentiments familiar from *Thyestes*. This is hardly surprising in the case of Andrugio, given that he, like Thyestes, is a former monarch who professes disdain for power's trappings. When Andrugio enters for the first time in Act 3 he is overwhelmed by misfortune and explicitly rejects philosophy, preferring to wallow in self-pity, choosing to fall upon the ground and beat it with his fists. It is his recollection of Senecan heroism, specifically Medea's famed assertion of her own survival and of the impotence of fortune to affect the mind (*Medea* 166, 176), which leads to Andrugio's adoption of positions akin to those of Thyestes and the Chorus in *Thyestes*. Thus 3.1 closes with Andrugio quoting Thyestes: 'No matter whither but from whence we fall' (*magis unde cadas quam quo refert*, 926). When he returns in 4.1, Andrugio asks for water in terms reminiscent of Thyestes' moralising on the danger of drinking from cups of gold (*Thyestes* 453):

> Give me water, boy;
> There is no poison in't I hope. They say
> That lurks in massy plate.
> *Antonio and Mellida* 4.1.35-7

He then continues with these reflections:

> 'Tis not the barèd pate, the bended knees,
> Gilt tipstaves, Tyrian purple, chairs of state,
> Troops of pied butterflies that flutter still
> In greatness' summer, that confirm a prince;
> 'Tis not the unsavoury breath of multitudes,
> Shouting and clapping with confusèd din,
> That makes a prince. No, Lucio, he's a king,
> A true right king, that dares do aught save wrong,
> Fears nothing mortal but to be unjust;
> Who is not blown up with the flattering puffs
> Of spongy sycophants; who stands unmoved
> Despite the jostling of opinion;
> Who can enjoy himself maugre the throng
> That strive to press his quiet out of him;
> Who sits upon Jove's footstool, as I do,
> Adoring, not affecting, majesty;
> Whose brow is wreathèd with the silver crown
> And of this empire every man's possessed
> That's worth his soul.
> *Antonio and Mellida* 4.1.45-65

These lines constitute an expanded paraphrase of the following lines from *Thyestes'* second choral ode (344-52, 388-90):

regem non faciunt opes,
non uestis Tyriae color,
non frontis nota regia,
non auro nitidae trabes:
rex est qui posuit metus
et diri mala pectoris;
quem non ambitio impotens
et numquam stabilis fauor
uulgi praecipitis mouet ...
rex est qui metuet nihil,
rex est qui cupiet nihil:
hoc regnum sibi quisque dat.

Wealth does not make a king, not colour of Tyrian garment, not brow's royal mark, not beams gleaming with gold: a king is one who has set aside fear and the perverse heart's evils; whom no uncontrolled ambition and never stable favour of the headlong mob affects ... A king is one who will fear nothing, a king is one who will desire nothing: each gives this kingdom to himself.

However, Andrugio's quotations from Seneca should not be viewed as evidence that he embodies Stoic virtue. Andrugio exits at the end of 3.1 apparently determined to put his former state behind him:

Well, ere yon sun set, I'll show myself,
Worthy my blood. I was a duke; that's all.

But his next words, 'No matter whither but from whence we fall', words drawn from Thyestes' drunken song (925f.), suggest not rejection of concern for status but its opposite. In similar fashion, the *Thyestes*-like homily on the value of philosophic kingship is immediately followed with a denunciation of the people of Genoa for their disloyalty and with an expression of regret over loss of power (4.1.67-83).[81] Andrugio apes not only Thyestes' moral sentiments but also his hypocrisy.

Given the Stoic notion that only the wise man is truly happy, we might expect that in a play which raises Senecan issues, a character called Felice might well be a philosopher. Certainly that is how the actor playing Felice conceives of his role in the Induction, for he describes his spirit as follows:

> 'Tis steady, and must seem so impregnably fortressed with his own content that no envious thought could ever invade his spirit; never surveying any man so unmeasuredly happy whom I thought not justly hateful for some true impoverishment; never beholding any favour of Madam Felicity gracing another, which his well-bounded content persuaded not to hang in the front of his own fortune; and therefore as far from envying any man as he valued all men infinitely distant from accomplished beatitude. These native adjuncts appropriate to me the name of Felice.
>
> *Antonio and Mellida*, Induction 100-8

And so we find that in the play's opening scene Felice plays the role of moralist in a manner analogous to that of the Minister in Act 2 of *Thyestes*, for Felice advances the claims of morality to oppose Piero's tyrannical assertions. Thus Felice warns Piero of the danger of pride (1.1.45ff.) and engages in a brief exchange reminiscent of the Nero-Seneca debate in *Octavia*, including a translation of line 465, and the Atreus-Minister debate in *Thyestes*, upon which it is modelled, including a paraphrase of 217f. But it is in Act 3, Scene 2 that Marston most clearly exploits *Thyestes*, for Felice begins by telling how he wanders through the court at night to see if he envies the felicity of others, reminding us of Thyestes' rejection of joining day with sleep and night with wine (466f.). He claims, like the wise man depicted in *Thyestes'* second choral ode (365f., 393-6), to look down on the world's misfortunes and to be content with an undistinguished life (3.2.41ff.). But when in the next speech Castilio announces his success in love, Felice immediately exposes his own envy, his lack of philosophical detachment.[82] His claims to Stoic virtue are as fraudulent as those of Thyestes and Andrugio.

If *Antonio and Mellida* treats Senecan issues in an unexpected genre, the play's sequel, *Antonio's Revenge*, exploits not only Senecan quotation but Senecan form, for, as its title suggests, this is revenge tragedy.

As *Antonio and Mellida* began with Piero's triumph, so too

does *Antonio's Revenge*,[83] for the tyrant enters exultant over his murder of the two would-be Stoics, Andrugio and Felice. And once again Marston underlines resemblances between Piero and Atreus, for just as Atreus can barely control his passions when Thyestes is within his grasp (496), so Piero 'can scarce coop triumphing vengeance up' (1.1.11). Moreover, Piero's resentment at Andrugio's success with Maria is reminiscent of Atreus' bitterness at the loss of Aerope to Thyestes. At least in these early scenes Piero continues his re-enactment of the role of Atreus.

The deaths of Andrugio and Felice, however, require a new representative of Stoic thought, a new substitute for Atreus' Minister, Thyestes and the Chorus. That task falls to Pandulfo, Felice's father, who asserts that he will 'talk as chorus to this tragedy' (1.2.298), claims indifference to his son's death in order to represent himself as embodying Stoic *apatheia* and quotes Seneca's *On Providence* to prove the point.[84] Even more telling is the fact that, like Felice, Pandulfo engages in a dialogue with Piero which recalls that between Atreus and his Minister in Act 2 of *Thyestes*:

Piero:	Where only honest deeds to kings are free
	It is no empire, but a beggary.
Pandulfo:	Where more than noble deeds to kings are free
	It is no empire, but a tyranny.
Piero:	Tush, juiceless greybeard, 'tis immunity
	Proper to princes that our state exacts,
	Our subjects not alone to bear, but praise our acts.
Pandulfo:	O, but that prince that worthful praise aspires,
	From hearts, and not from lips, applause desires.
Piero:	Pish! True praise the brow of common men doth ring,
	False only girts the temple of a king.
	He that hath strength and's ignorant of power,
	He was not made to rule, but to be ruled.
Pandulfo:	'Tis praise to do not what we can but should.
Piero:	Hence, doting stoic!

Antonio's Revenge 2.1.119-33

Piero's argument that rulers should not be bound by moral concerns recalls Atreus' similar rejection of morality (214f.), while the debate over the value of praise translates the dispute between Atreus and his Minister (*Thyestes* 205-12):

Atreus: maximum hoc regni bonum est,
                  quod facta domini cogitur populus sui
                  tam ferre quam laudare.
Satelles: quos cogit metus
                  laudare, eosdem reddit inimicos metus.
                  at qui fauoris gloriam ueri petit,
                  animo magis quam uoce laudari uolet.
Atreus: laus uera et humili saepe contingit uiro,
                  non nisi potenti falsa.

Atreus: This is kingship's greatest good,
                  That the people are forced to suffer
                  As much as praise their master's deeds.
Minister: Whom fear compels
                  To praise, fear makes hostile.
                  But he who seeks the glory of true support,
                  Will want to be praised in heart as much as voice.
Atreus: True praise often befalls the lowly,
                  False only the powerful.

Although Piero and Pandulfo echo their ancient forebears, it is not clear that this debate produces the same result, for Pandulfo goes on to defy the tyrant, while Atreus' Minister retreats in fear.

But if Pandulfo can sustain Stoic fortitude in the face of his son's death, Antonio feels otherwise, for in the next scene he enters holding a text of Seneca. Antonio begins by quoting one of Seneca's great avengers, Medea: 'Pigmy cares / can shelter under patience' shield, but giant griefs / Will burst all covert' (2.2.4-6).[85] Some forty lines later, he reads in Latin some slightly adapted lines from Seneca's *On Providence*:

Endure with courage: this is the way in which you surpass god. He is exempt from suffering misfortune; you are above it. Despise grief: either it will be dissolved, or it will dissolve you. Despise fortune: it has no weapon with which to strike your soul.

106

In their original context these are the imagined words of god responding to human complaint about the sorrows of this world. They also constitute the rationale for Pandulfo's response to his son's death, for he cites them in translation at 1.2.334f. For Antonio these words are nonsense: 'Pish! Thy mother was not lately widowed, / Thy dear affièd love lately defamed / With blemish of foul lust when thou wrot'st thus' (2.2.50-2). For Antonio Seneca defines the two possible reactions to his father's death and the slandering of Mellida: the endurance recommended by the philosopher and the vengeance presented in the tragedies. It is tragic Seneca that Antonio takes as guide. The point is further underlined by Antonio's quotation of the Latin words of Agrippina's vengeful ghost from *Octavia*:[86] 'Ah, where has my labour, where have my words fallen?' (2.2.153).

In Act 3 Antonio takes on a variety of Thyestean roles. First he summons up Andrugio's ghost. Now the ghost plays a role akin to that of the Fury in Act 1 of *Thyestes*, inciting Antonio to revenge, reminding him of Atreus' axiom: *scelera non ulcisceris, nisi uincis* ('You do not avenge crimes, unless you surpass them', *Thyestes* 196), while Antonio plays the role of Tantalus' ghost, quoting in Latin and combining with slight variation two of Tantalus' speeches from the prologue:

> o quisquis noua
> supplicia functis durus umbrarum arbiter
> disponis ... quisquis exeso iaces
> pauidus sub antro iamque uenturi times
> montis ruinam, quisquis auidorum feros
> rictus leonum et dira Furiarum agmina
> implicitus horres, *Antonii* uocem excipe
> properantis ad uos: *ulciscar*.
> 3.2.66-73; *Thyestes* 13-15, 75-81; Marston's alterations italicised

Harsh judge of ghosts, whoever you are, who allocate fresh punishments to the dead ... whoever you are who lie in fear beneath the hollowed cave and already fear the mountain's imminent collapse, whoever shudders at the savage jaws of greedy lions and, entangled, at grim columns of Furies, hear the voice *of Antonio* hastening towards you: *I will be avenged.*

Not only does Antonio speak Tantalus' words, but he inserts his name into the ghost's speech, replacing Tantalus' name with his own. Antonio becomes Tantalus.

It is, however, the advent of Piero's son, Julio, which leads Antonio to play an even more significant Senecan role, the role of Atreus. The change is marked by Antonio adapting the words of Atreus as he catches sight of Thyestes with his sons. Where Atreus said *uenit in nostras manus / tandem Thyestes, uenit, et totus quidem* (494f., 'At last Thyestes has come into our hands, he has come, yes, all of him'), Antonio says *Venit in nostras manus / Tandem uindicta, uenit et tota quidem* (3.2.151f., 'At last vengeance has come into our hands, it has come, yes, all of it'). Like Atreus, Antonio sees himself as surpassing Jove (3.2.161ff.) and like Atreus, Antonio parodies religious ritual, for where Atreus' murder of Thyestes' children perverts Greco-Roman sacrificial practice, Antonio's destruction of Julio, particularly the sprinkling of his blood upon Andrugio's tomb, burlesques the requiem mass (3.2.205f.).[87] Even Julio's willing death (3.2.186) recalls young Tantalus' refusal to protest against his fate (720f.). The transformation of Antonio into Atreus is underlined by the stage-direction immediately following 3.3.72, which recalls Piero's Atreus-like entry in 1.1, and his godlike exultation at 3.3.77ff.:

> O, my soul's enthroned
> In the triumphant chariot of revenge,
> Methinks I am all air and feel no weight
> Of human dirt clog.
>
> *Antonio's Revenge* 3.3.77-80

Antonio has now become Medea, who actually does hover above the stage in 'triumphant chariot' in Seneca's play; has become Atreus, who in his own mind at least achieves apotheosis (885f., 911). But Antonio's most Atreid moment occurs in Act 5 when he presents to Piero the body of his son to feast upon, indulging in that verbal play which is characteristic of the Argive king:

Here lies a dish to feast thy father's gorge;
Here's flesh and blood which I am sure thou lov'st.
                                    Antonio's Revenge 5.3.80f.

Antonio has become Atreus in word and deed.

By contrast Piero, who is initially presented as a second Atreus and who subsequently views himself as another of Seneca's great revengers, Clytemnestra, for he quotes her at 2.2.221,[88] has now become Thyestes, the man whose craving for power destroys him, for Piero loses his son, his tongue, his life.

But even more remarkable than the transformations of Antonio and Piero is the metamorphosis of Pandulfo. As I observed earlier, Pandulfo is explicitly set up as the play's spokesman for Stoic values, playing the roles of Chorus and of Atreus' Minister from *Thyestes* and quoting from Seneca's *On Providence* (1.2.334f.). He even puts Stoicism into practice when he refuses to mourn his son: 'Why therefore should I weep?' (1.2.296). In Act 4 we still find Pandulfo citing Seneca's philosophical works in Latin and in English. It is, however, the sight of Felice's body that puts an end to Pandulfo's *apatheia*:

Alberto:	You have lost a good son.
Pandulfo:	Why there's the comfort on't, that he was good.
	Alas, poor innocent!
Alberto:	Why weeps mine uncle?
Pandulfo:	Ha? Dost ask me why? Ha? Ha?
	Good coz, look here.
	He shows him his son's breast
	Man will break out despite philosophy.
	Why, all this while I ha' but played a part
	Like to some boy that acts a tragedy ...

                                    Antonio's Revenge 4.2.64-71

It is in these lines that we see Pandulfo change, for he enters this exchange finding comfort in Felice's goodness but closes with the recognition that his philosophy was all pretence. His tears, his laughter mark the loss of that rational self-control which philosophy enjoins.

From this point on Pandulfo becomes more Atreus-like than

Antonio himself. It is Pandulfo who suggests the cutting out of Piero's tongue.[89] And just as it is the sight of Thyestes' grief which leads Atreus to his cry of satisfaction *nunc meas laudo manus ... perdideram scelus, / nisi sic doleres* (1096-98, 'now I glorify my hands ... I had lost my crime, if you did not grieve so'), so the sight of the bleeding Piero leads Pandulfo to exclaim 'He weeps! Now do I glorify my hands; / I had no vengeance if I had no tears' (5.3.76f.).[90] Pandulfo even echoes Atreus' concern for legitimacy of his sons. Where Atreus reacts to Thyestes' concern about eating his own children with an assertion that Agamemnon and Menelaus are truly his (*certos*, 1102), Pandulfo responds to Piero's grief with the hope that Julio truly was Piero's son (5.3.93-6). The philosopher proves just as vicious as Antonio.

Although the endings of *Thyestes* and *Antonio's Revenge* are strikingly different, the plays have this in common: they present revengers as unreservedly successful. Thyestes entrusts Atreus' punishment to the gods in a world from which the gods have fled, only to be capped by Atreus' superb reply: 'I entrust you for punishment to your children.' In Marston's play it is not the gods who are at issue but the relationship between the revengers and the rest of society. When Antonio, Pandulfo and Alberto have finished stabbing Piero, various Venetians enter, including two senators. Where we might expect these embodiments of state power to disapprove of such bloody acts, in fact they bless the killers' deeds and offer Antonio wealth and dignity.

Senecan prose, with its unreserved condemnation of anger and revenge, and Senecan tragedy, with its powerful representation of the lust for bloody retribution, define issues central to the *Antonio* plays, for Marston is concerned with the relationship between reason and emotion, with the possibility that adherence to philosophic norms might limit or control the human propensity to violence. *Thyestes* in particular constitutes a reference point for the understanding of Marston's dramas, for even in these very different plays the characters find themselves re-enacting, whether consciously or not, roles once defined in Roman tragedy.

4. Reception

Jonson's *Sejanus His Fall*[91] exploits a wide variety of ancient texts, its subject matter being drawn from Roman imperial history and its principal narrative sources being the historians Tacitus, Suetonius, Dio Cassius and the satirist Juvenal. Jonson even goes so far as to quote a favoured saying of Tiberius in Greek (2.330), neatly rhyming 'fury' with *puri* ('fire'). In addition, the play's form is broadly classical, being divided into five acts and favouring narrative over direct representation for its depiction of the destruction of Sejanus and his family. On the other hand, as Jonson observed in his address 'To the Readers', *Sejanus* does not include a chorus and does not observe unity of time. In form at least, Jonson's play is less classical, less Senecan, than other Renaissance plays.

Nevertheless, Jonson does exploit Senecan tragedy, especially *Thyestes*, in this play, using the spectators' familiarity with Atreus to establish the true nature of Sejanus' aspirations. After the extraordinary exchanges between Sejanus, Eudemus and Livia which open Act 2, Sejanus enters after line 138 speaking of the revenge he will achieve by corrupting Livia:

> Adultery? It is the lightest ill,
> I will commit. A race of wicked acts
> Shall flow out of my anger, and o'erspread
> The world's wide face, which no posterity
> Shall ever approve, nor yet keep silent; things
> That for their cunning, close, and cruel mark,
> Thy father would wish his ...
>
> *Sejanus* 2.150-6

As commentators point out, these lines recall Atreus' first speech, the speech in which he stirs himself to seek revenge (*Thyestes* 192-5):

> age, anime, fac quod nulla posteritas probet,
> sed nulla taceat. aliquod audendum est nefas
> atrox, cruentum, tale quod frater meus
> suum esse mallet ...

Come now, my soul, perform a deed which no posterity could approve, nor yet keep silent. Some crime must be dared, dreadful, bloody, such that my brother would wish his ...

With these lines Jonson seems to mark out Sejanus as an aspiring Atreus. That reading is confirmed by Jonson's next scene, for the Tiberius-Sejanus meeting recalls the Atreus-Minister debate. But where Seneca presents the ruler as contemptuous of moral values, in Jonson it the monarch's servant who contemns morality. Both Atreus' Minister (216) and Tiberius (2.176) profess concern for cardinal Roman values, while Atreus and Sejanus value power above all (217f./2.180ff.). Even more tellingly, both Atreus and Sejanus believe in the value of unwilling praise. Where Atreus claims (*Thyestes* 205-7):

> maximum hoc regni bonum est,
> quod facta domini cogitur populus sui
> tam ferre quam laudare.

This is kingship's greatest good, that the people are forced to suffer as much as praise their master's deeds.

Sejanus asserts:

> All modesty is fond; and chiefly where
> The subject is no less compelled to bear,
> Than praise his sov'reign's acts.
>
> *Sejanus* 2.276-8

Here Jonson gives us, it seems, not Seneca repeated, but Seneca reversed: a moral monarch in debate with a cynical servant. At least, that is how it appears until Tiberius reveals his hand:

> We can no longer
> Keep on our mask to thee, our dear Sejanus;
> Thy thoughts are ours, in all ...
>
> *Sejanus* 2.278-80

4. Reception

In one sense, the resemblance between the two scenes is misleading, for Tiberius is not engaging in genuine debate: his true concern is not to advance morality's claims but to test his agent. In another sense, however, the resemblance is important, for allusion to *Thyestes* points up the fact that *Sejanus* has two Atreus-like figures, one actual and one aspiring.

The association between Atreus and Sejanus is reinforced in Sejanus' entry-speech in Act 5.

> My roof receives me not; 'tis air I tread –
> And, at each step, I feel my advancèd head
> Knock out a star in heav'n!
>
> *Sejanus* 5.7-9

The parallel with Atreus' first words in Act 5 of *Thyestes* seems patent (885f.):

> aequalis astris gradior et cunctos super
> altum superbo uertice attingens polum.
>
> Equal to the stars I walk and above all, touching the lofty sky with my proud head.

In each case the words express the speaker's joy in achieving his ambitions: Atreus' craving for revenge against his brother and Sejanus' desire for consent to marry Livia. But Sejanus' words seem curiously banal.[92] Like Atreus, he 'walks tall', but Sejanus' language, particularly his reference to the roof, to walking on air and to knocking stars from heaven, presses the metaphor to the point of absurdity.

But this is not the only time Sejanus explores this idea of knocking stars from heaven, for after Macro pledges loyalty, Sejanus denounces fear and calls upon the gods to witness his declaration in these terms:

> By you, that fools call gods,
> Hang all the sky with your prodigious signs,
> Fill earth with monsters, drop the scorpion down

Shake off the loosened globe from her long hinge,
Roll all the world in darkness ...

Sejanus 5.390-5

As commentators duly note, reference to the zodiac's collapse
and to the world's envelopment in darkness clearly alludes to
the sun's response to Atreus' crime reported by *Thyestes'*
Messenger (776ff.) and to the Chorus's description of the
constellations' fall in *Thyestes'* fourth ode. But the events
offered by Sejanus either as an impossibility (this unlikely event
will happen before I feel fear) or as a wish (may this dread event
occur if I feel fear), are presented in *Thyestes* as in some sense
actual. Allusion to the Roman play suggests that Sejanus'
bravado is misplaced. And so it is, for Macro's pledge of loyalty
is false and the would-be tyrant is outsmarted by the play's true
Atreus, the emperor Tiberius. Sejanus' quotations from
Thyestes underline both his ambitions and his folly.

Although *Sejanus* was by no means a popular success,
Jonson returned to material drawn from Roman history, and
observed classical norms even more strictly in *Catiline His
Conspiracy*,[93] for now he used choral odes as well as five-act
form. Although the combination of five acts and intervening
choruses undoubtedly makes *Catiline* more Senecan in appearance, it should be noted that in having the Chorus intervene in
the play's action in Acts 3 and 4, Jonson followed Greek rather
than Roman precedent.[94] The play's subject matter is also
distinctly unSenecan, for it presents not a royal court controlled
by an absolute monarch, but the chaotic and competitive world
of Roman republican politics. In that respect *Catiline* has little
in common with either *Sejanus* or *Thyestes*.[95] Hence it is not
surprising that Jonson alludes primarily to *Thyestes'* first Act,
and that it is not Atreus who is important for *Catiline*, but the
Fury and Tantalus' ghost.

The play begins with a ghostly prologue in a manner reminiscent of Seneca's *Agamemnon* and *Thyestes*. In so far as there
are two persons on stage, Sylla's ghost and Catiline,[96] the
prologue more closely resembles *Thyestes*; in so far the ghost is

effectively alone (there is no interaction between Sylla's ghost and Catiline) it more closely resembles *Agamemnon*. Be that as it may, Sylla's ghost quotes from *Thyestes*, not *Agamemnon* (lines 11-15 translate *Thyestes* 87-9; lines 55-63 include *Thyestes* 29-32, 48f.). The connection is confirmed in the following exchange from Act 1:

Longinus: A strange, unwonted horror doth invade me,
               I know not what it is!
                      A darkness comes over the place.
Lecca: The day goes back,
            Or else my senses!
Curius: As at Atreus' feast!
                                 Catiline 1.311-13

If we note that Longinus' words recall those of Atreus plotting with his Minister (260ff., 267ff.), we might conclude that Jonson suggests an equivalence between Catiline's plotting against legitimate authority and the crimes of Atreus. The parallel, however, is not sustained in subsequent acts. Comparison with the plays which we have considered and are about to consider suggests that allusion to *Thyestes* is not intrinsic to *Catiline's* dramatic structure.

That Seneca's *Thyestes* was an important model for Elizabethan and Jacobean drama, particularly revenge tragedy, is widely accepted. We can go further: encountering *Thyestes* produced a wide variety of responses in Renaissance England, including the exploitation of Senecan form and themes, radical transformation and sophisticated intertextual engagement.

Thyestes in Renaissance Italy and France: two plays

It was not only in England that dramatists were exploiting *Thyestes*, for Seneca was no less important in Italy and France in the sixteenth century.[97] By way of illustration, I propose to examine briefly two major plays by important dramatists, Giraldi Cinzio's *Orbecche* (1541) and Robert Garnier's *Les Juifves* (1583).

Giovan Battista Giraldi Cinzio's *Orbecche*, first performed in Ferrara in 1541, is one of the earliest plays to exploit *Thyestes*.[98] Although the subject of Cinzio's play is not classical in origin, being drawn from one of his own *novelle*, the drama's structure is Senecan, for he employs five-act form (five acts, four choral odes), observes the unities of time and plot and prefers to narrate rather than stage the play's most violent actions. His use of direct address to the spectators in a prologue, however, is more characteristic of ancient comedy than tragedy.

Cinzio draws attention to his awareness of *Thyestes* through allusion to the history of the Tantalid house (1.1.97; 1.2.49; 4.1.25f.) and by the use of such motifs as the darkening of the sun and the flight of the world's vegetation (1.1.127-30). More importantly, the play's first act, which involves Nemesis and the three Furies in the first scene and the ghost of Selina in the second, is modelled on the first act of *Thyestes*; the counselling scene between tyrant and adviser (3.2) rewrites Act 2 of *Thyestes*; while the Messenger's narrative in Act 4 is based on the Messenger's narrative in *Thyestes* Act 4.[99]

Where *Thyestes'* first Act presents an encounter between a Fury and an ancestor, Tantalus, Act 1 of *Orbecche* gives us a first scene involving the goddess Nemesis and the three Furies and a second scene with a solitary ancestor, Selina, former wife of the Persian king, Sulmone. Nemesis begins with a statement of Christian doctrine, asserting first, that goodness is rewarded and that wickedness is punished (1.1.39f.) and, secondly, that guilt can be inherited and punished in later generations (1.1.42-4). This is plainly intended to justify her plan to punish Sulmone along with the innocent members of his family. To achieve this, she summons all three Furies and orders them to fill Sulmone's court with grief, torment, crying and death (1.1.115f.). This they do. Thus Nemesis re-enacts the part of *Thyestes'* Fury, but in a manner which does not compromise divine goodness.

In the second scene, Selina, dead mother of Orbecche, enters, angered that Nemesis has already aroused the Furies against the house. Indeed, Selina's role is also like that of Seneca's

Fury, for she predicts events to come: Sulmone's murder of Orbecche's husband and sons; Orbecche's killing of Sulmone and her suicide; and their assignment to hell along with Tantalus, Tityos, Ixion and Sisyphus, the familiar Senecan sinners. Selina also plays the role of criminal ancestor (Sulmone killed her for incest with her son) and so combines the roles of Seneca's Fury and Tantalus. Thus Cinzio has rearranged his Senecan material, reassigning roles, it seems, to accommodate Christian teaching, with Nemesis as representative of divine justice and Selina as agent for sheer revenge.

If Act 1 significantly reworks the first Act of *Thyestes*, *Orbecche's* third act reshapes material from *Thyestes* Act 2, introducing the play's tyrant and marking him out as a ruler of Atreid qualities. The second and third scenes in Act 2, reshape material from *Thyestes*. In 3.2 one of the king's ministers, Malecche, attempts to restrain the Sulmone's impulse to anger. *Orbecche* differs strikingly from *Thyestes* in that the Minister seems to succeed, with the king finally declaring that he is willing to do what Malecche asks (3.2.345). It is not until Scene 3 that Sulmone reveals his true nature in a soliloquy in which he reveals that he believes that death is not punishment, but the end of punishment (51-3; cf. *Thyestes* 246) and that it is characteristic of a king that his guilty deeds are praised by all (70f.; cf. *Thyestes* 205-7). The scene ends with Sulmone joyfully watching the entry of his victims and expressing the need for self-restraint (77-81; cf. *Thyestes* 496, 504f.).

Sulmone's crime, the killing of Oronte and his children, is also presented in Thyestean terms. Cinzio's Messenger begins by wishing that he had been born elsewhere, listing a variety of foreign places, as Seneca's begins by expressing disbelief that such savagery could occurred in a civilised place and not some foreign land.[100] Indeed the Messenger refers to Atreus and Thyestes (4.1.25f.) and declares that the sun and moon should be blotted out (4.1.51f.). Now comes the description of the murder of the three victims with emphasis on the tyrant's brutal wit, most notably in the cutting off of Oronte's hands with the words: 'This / is the sceptre I offer you, in this way / I want to make you king. Are you content with this?' (82-4). We are then told how Sulmone slit the first child's throat and killed both second son and father in a single blow. Even more telling than these vivid descriptions is the use of images derived from *Thyestes*, for Sulmone is likened to a hound (139, cf. *Thyestes* 497ff.), a lion (218, cf. *Thyestes* 732ff.) and a tiger (227, cf. *Thyestes* 707ff.). Finally, the bodies are prepared for presentation to Orbecche in Act 5.

From Cinzio's handling of the first act and his representation of Sulmone, it is clear that *Thyestes* is an important intertext for *Orbecche*. However, the Italian playwright has set his Atreus-like tyrant in a wholly different context, a world ruled by divine providence, a world in which the tyrant's cruelty is stoutly resisted, a world in which the tyrant's punishment is promised by Nemesis in Act 1 and is realised by his daughter in Act 5. Unlike Atreus, Sulmone is punished for his crimes.

Robert Garnier is generally regarded as the finest of French Renaissance dramatists and *Les Juifves* (1583) is considered his masterpiece.[101] As its name suggests, the play's subject matter, though ancient, is not classical, with Garnier citing as his sources the *Fourth Book of Kings* chs 24 and 25, the *Second Book of Chronicles* ch. 36, *Jeremiah* ch. 29 and Josephus *Jewish Antiquities* 10.9-10.[102] But if Garnier's subject matter derives from the Hebrew Bible and Josephus, the play's dramaturgy shows familiarity with Senecan tragedy, for Garnier employs the familiar five-act structure with intervening choruses.[103]

The two primary non-Biblical intertexts for *Les Juifves* are Seneca's *Trojan Women* and *Thyestes*.[104] Amital, mother of king Sédécie, combining as she does the roles of former queen and Chorus-leader, most closely resembles Seneca's Hecuba; the Prevost, who persuades the wives of Sédécie into handing over their children, plays a role analogous to that of Ulysses in *Trojan Women*, while the two female Choruses remind us of Seneca's Chorus of lamenting Trojan women. It is the play's tyrant, Nabuchodonosor, who makes plain Garnier's use of *Thyestes*, for each time he enters the stage, at the beginning of Acts 2 and 3 and in the course of Act 4, he begins by quoting Atreus.

4. Reception

Act 2 begins with Nabuchodonosor's words: *Pareil aux Dieux je marche* (181, 'Equal to the gods I walk'), words which virtually translate Atreus' first words in Act 5: *aequalis astris gradior* (885, 'Equal to the stars I walk'). Like Atreus, Nabuchodonosor claims equality with the gods. But where Atreus is alone, Nabuchodonosor is accompanied by his general, Nabuzardan, and Nabuchodonosor's speech is not followed by the revelation of his victim, but by a debate over the nature of punishment. It seems, then, that we are to have a re-enactment of the Atreus-Minister debate from *Thyestes*, Act 2.

And so it proves. Like Atreus, the Assyrian king wants to punish his enemy. Like the Minister, Nabuzardan opposes further penalties, arguing that Sédécie's humiliation is enough (217, 219-22). But the reasons given are unexpected. In the first part of this scene Nabuzardan's position resembles that of Atreus, while Nabuchodonosor's parallels that of his Minister, for Nabuzardan argues that to leave Sédécie alive is the more effective punishment (219-22), while Nabuchodonosor sees death as the greatest penalty. Moreover, the reasons Nabuzardan gives are Atreus-like, for he claims that to kill one's enemy is to lose all vengeance (227f.), asserts that Sédécie should be forced to live precisely because he wants to die (230) and argues that death would free the Jewish king from suffering (232-8). In the first part of this scene Garnier gives us not Seneca, but Seneca in reverse: a tyrant who sees death as a satisfying penalty and a minister who argues that mercy is the more exquisite form of punishment.

But by the scene's end the picture has become more complex, for Nabuzardan shifts his ground, now arguing that a king should restrain his anger (268-71) and that excess in punishment renders a ruler inhuman (273-9). It turns out that Nabuzardan genuinely advocates clemency. How then do we explain his previous Atreus-like stance? Perhaps he was employing the kind of argument for mercy which he thought would appeal to Nabuchodonosor. But however we judge Nabuzardan, one thing is clear: in Act 2 Nabuchodonosor is a tyrant who is yet to understand tyranny's true nature.

When he enters in Act 3, the Assyrian king echoes Atreus' gloating description of Thyestes in Act 3. Where Atreus declared: *plagis tenetur clausa dispositis fera* (491, 'the beast is held by the traps we set'), Nabuchodonosor claims: *Je le tiens je le tiens, je tiens la beste prise* (887, 'I hold him, I hold him, I hold the beast I caught'). And both Atreus and Nabuchodonosor continue to employ the language of the hunt. Once again, Atreus is effectively alone, for his speech is a soliloquy, and, once again, Nabuchodonosor is accompanied, this time by his wife. Here too, the characters are concerned with the nature of punishment. But now the Assyrian king advances the same argument as the Argive monarch, for, though opposing mercy, Nabuchodonosor proposes to keep Sédécie alive (956). After the queen's exit, Nabuchodonosor declares to the audience that although the Jewish king will live, he will pray for death to end his tortures (963-74). Nabuchodonosor has become another Atreus.

In Act 4 Nabuchodonosor enters when Sédécie and the high priest, Sarrée, are already on stage. At first, however, he does not notice their presence and so the king begins with an Atreus-like soliloquy:

> Should I be so weak and slack in heart, so feeble in courage towards my enemies, remaining without vengeance and betraying the glory and the sweet fruit of such a victory?
> *Les Juifves* 1361-4

With these words Nabuchodonosor recalls Atreus' first outburst of self-reproach, the first words he uttered on stage (176ff.). In the debate (or rather exchange of abuse) between Nabuchodonosor and Sédécie which follows, the Jewish king acknowledges his guilt and dares his captor to do his worst. It is in Act 5 that we learn what constitutes Nabuchodonosor's worst, for the prophet announces to Amital and Sédécie's wives the decapitation of the chief priest, the murder of Sédécie's children before his eyes, and his blinding. Although Garnier's description of the tyrant's cruelties is more restrained than Seneca's, we can accept that his Nabuchodonosor is a true descendant of Atreus, for both child-killers remain unmoved by their grisly deeds (*Thyestes* 704; *Les Juifves* 1937). Garnier's use of *Thyestes* in *Les Juifves* is subtle, complex and unmistakable.

Adapting *Thyestes*: from the seventeenth to the twentieth century

Many classical myths, those concerning the Trojan war, for example, or the later generations of the house of Atreus (Agamemnon and Clytemnestra, Orestes and Electra) or individuals like Medea, Phaedra, Alcestis, and Orpheus recur frequently in drama, opera and even film. By contrast, the story of Atreus and Thyestes has proved one of the least popular for adaptation on the European stage. Despite the close engagement of Renaissance dramatists with Seneca's text and with Senecan issues, subsequent playwrights have, for the most part, attempted to strip the myth of its terrifying power. It was not until the second half of the twentieth century that a major dramatist was able to treat this myth with a vigour and an urgency comparable to Seneca's.

The earliest English work explicitly to rewrite the Thyestes-myth was not a tragedy but a comedy, or rather a parody attached to a translation. In 1674 John Wright, an otherwise unknown barrister,[105] published THYESTES A Tragedy, *Translated out of Seneca: To which is Added* MOCK-THYESTES, IN BURLESQUE, dedicating the work to the Right Honourable Bennet LORD Sherard.[106] In his Advertisement Wright claims that his translation had been written many years previously but that he had revised it at leisure in the country, a pastime more agreeable than 'the continual Glut of Ale and Tobacco'. He gives no indication as to when the parody was written.[107]

Wright's *Mock Thyestes*, though written in verse little better than doggerel, mimics the structure of Seneca's original, being written in five acts with four intervening choruses and disposing its material in a similar way. Act 1 presents an encounter between Tantalus and Megaera, in which Tantalus complains of being aroused from his rest and argues that humans are so corrupt that there is no point in his returning. Since Tantalus resists, Megaera threatens to whip his buttocks. Tantalus yields. At this point the Chorus relates a trivialised history of the house of Tantalus with events being transferred from Greece to London. Act 2, as one might expect, presents a debate between Atreus and a servant, in which Atreus argues that his wife was so lacking in beauty that Thyestes can only have committed adultery with her for reasons of spite. When asked how Thyestes should be punished, the servant suggests gelding. Atreus rejects the proposal for fear of a lawsuit. The servant then proposes that Atreus debauch Thyestes' wife when he eventually marries. This proposal is rejected as being too dilatory. The act closes with the proposal to send a letter to Thyestes. In Ode 2 the Chorus denounces the brothers for quarrelling over so trifling a matter as 'a little Cuckolding'. Act 3 has Thyestes entering with a bag in hand and considering whether he should stay or go, wondering if he will be received with blows or feasting. When the brothers meet, Thyestes asks (somewhat tactlessly) after Atreus' wife and children, while Atreus asks about the welfare of Thyestes' cats. As it happens, they are in Thyestes' bag. Atreus leaves with the intention of organising dinner. Ode 3 follows with reflections on the quicksilver nature of quarrels within families. In Act 4 the Messenger praises Thyestes' cats and his fondness for them. We are then told how Atreus killed the cats, divided them to be cooked in different styles, and served them to his brother. A mock star-Chorus follows. The play closes with Thyestes' drunken song and Atreus' revelation that Thyestes has eaten his cats.

If John Wright was and is obscure, the author of the first English stage-play to be based upon *Thyestes*, John Crowne (?1640-?1703), was one of the most prominent and prolific of Restoration dramatists. Although Crowne is perhaps best known for his comedies, he also wrote a number of tragedies. Of these *Thyestes* is said to have met 'with good success' when first performed at the Theatre Royal in March 1681.[108]

Although clearly modelled on the Roman play, some lines

being translated from Seneca's Latin, Crowne's *Thyestes* differs considerably from its archetype in plot and structure. Examination of the list of characters reveals significant differences. First, Crowne has increased the number of women characters. (In Seneca the Fury alone is female.) Now Atreus has a daughter, Antigone, a hitherto unknown sister for Agamemnon and Menelaus; Atreus' wife, Aerope, also plays a significant role. Secondly, where Seneca's Thyestes had three sons, Crowne's has only one, Philisthenes. These two changes point to a major difference between the two plays: Crowne's version incorporates a love plot, for Antigone and Philisthenes are betrothed. Indeed, Thyestes' meal forms part of their wedding banquet. Although employing Seneca's (by now conventional) five-act structure, Crowne's material is differently disposed. There is of course no Chorus, and the action takes place in various locations including the forecourt of the Argive palace, Thyestes' forest dwelling and Aerope's prison cell.

For a dramatist writing in a period of monarchical rule, particularly at a time when the monarch's power was fiercely contested, the subject of Atreus and Thyestes must have posed significant problems, for this is a myth in which a king is presented as an unabashed tyrant. The story's anti-royalist potential is obvious. The difficulty must have been particularly acute for Crowne, because the evidence, such as it is, points to him being a supporter of Charles II in his struggle against Parliament.[109] It is perhaps for this reason that where Seneca emphasised the drive for power as a motivating force, Crowne stresses sexual passion.[110] From the very start Atreus is presented as a maniacal murderer with an obsession for revenge. However, it immediately becomes clear that this obsession arises primarily from his belief that Aerope has willingly committed adultery with his brother. Thus when Antigone enters in Act 1 we have the following exchange:

Atreus:	Now! What art thou?
Antigone:	Antigone!
Atreus:	What's that?
Antigone:	Your daughter, sir.

123

Atreus: And are you sure of that?
By heavens, thy mother was so rank a whore,
That it is more than all the gods can tell
What share of thee is mine.

Crowne *Thyestes* p. 21

As in Seneca's play, Atreus is concerned with his children's paternity, but here the emphasis is less on the children and more on Aerope's apparent lack of chastity. The word 'whore' is constantly on Atreus' lips. We are told by Thyestes that before his adultery with Aerope, Atreus had been 'the best of Kings, and brothers' (p. 54) and can reasonably infer that it is this event which has corrupted Atreus. Thus we find emphasis on the king's past and present love for Aerope: 'Oh! How I lov'd that woman' (p. 22), 'that cursed woman, / Whom yet I love' (p. 23). But we also see and hear enough to infer that Aerope is guiltless. We see her protest her innocence, claiming that she was 'brutishly forc'd' (p. 43). We see madness come upon her at the mere thought of the vile accusations against her ('My wits are going; when I think of this / They always leave me', p. 43) and her hostility to the prospect of Thyestes' return to Argos. And it is she who kills Thyestes in Act 5. But even though Aerope denounces Thyestes to his face in Act 4, Atreus sees only evidence of her guilt: 'By the eternal gods, the whore commits / Incest in fancy with the villain here' (p. 60f.). And when Thyestes finally curses his brother declaring that his villainy has terrified the sun, Atreus declares that the sun 'cou'd lend all / His wealth to help thee corrupt my wife' (p. 72). Moreover, the primacy of sexual as opposed to political motivation is underlined by the fact that the play presents not a coronation scene (as in Act 3 of Seneca's play), but a failed coronation scene, for Thyestes does indeed reject the crown. The contest between the brothers is not political.

Turning *Thyestes* into an essentially domestic drama is, I suggest, one way of defusing the play's political potential, because it helps occlude the possibility of the drama being read as allegory. In terms of personal relationships there seems to be

virtually no resemblance between Charles II and Atreus, queen
Catherine and Aerope, James and Thyestes.

On the other hand, occasional lines might well be read as
having political import. Thus Atreus' question 'Can baseborn
bastards, lawful sovereigns be?' (p. 79) could be interpreted as
supporting the Charles II's view of the succession issue, in
particular, his support for his brother James over the bastard
Monmouth. More telling is the play's explicit hostility to
Catholicism. Thus the Prologue attacks 'cunning Romish
priests', while the Epilogue asserts that 'pagan and popish
priests / Are but two names for the same bloody beasts'.
Philisthenes goes further and suggests that priests are a threat
to the monarchy:

> And should the people enter into leagues,
> And vow the king to the infernal gods,
> For money you would aid their hellish vows,
> And curse all honest men that would not aid.
>
> *Thyestes* Act 4, p. 62f.

We might well see these lines as suggesting that the king avoid
too close an association with the Roman church. Crowne's
Thyestes is not wholly apolitical.[111]

Prosper Jolyot de Crébillon *père* (1675-1762) was the most
eminent tragedian in eighteenth-century France. *Atrée et
Thyeste*, his second surviving play, was first performed on 14
March 1707. Although the play's first performance seems to be
have been greeted with horror, with audiences finding the
presentation to Thyeste of a cup of his son's blood shocking in
the extreme, it was revived successfully in 1712.[112] Although
Atrée et Thyeste incorporates a number of Senecan lines,[113] the
plot is very different, as a glance at the list of characters
suggests: as well as Atrée and Thyeste, we find also Plisthène,
here the son of Thyeste and Aerope, though believed to be
Atrée's son, and Théodamie, daughter of Thyeste. In addition,
Atrée, Plisthène and Théodamie all have confidants. A further
difference is that the play is set not in Argos, but Chalcis,
capital of the island of Euboea.

As with Crowne's *Thyestes*, *Atrée et Thyeste* is essentially a domestic drama, for the issue of kingship does not arise. Thyeste's adultery with Aerope is now an event which took place twenty years ago. Nevertheless, as the play begins, Atrée is planning to send his fleet against Athens, Thyeste's place of exile, in order to punish the man who seduced his wife and fathered a child, Plisthène, whom all believe to be Atrée's. Here there is no question of Aerope being innocent: Atrée tells us that she died still in love with Thyeste and her letter establishes the truth of this claim (p. 52).

Perhaps the most interesting change effected by Crébillon is having Plisthène, son of Thyeste, thought to be Atrée's son. This misunderstanding enables Atrée to plan not only Thyeste's death, but death at his son's hands. Thus the audience has the prospect not merely of murder, but of unwitting parricide (p. 53). However, Plisthène foils this aspect of Atrée's plan by refusing to murder Thyeste: *Je serai son vainqueur, et non pas son bourreau* ('I will be his conqueror, but not his executioner', p. 55). But if this danger is avoided, another arises when we learn that Plisthène has fallen in love with a shipwrecked stranger who turns out to be Théodamie, Thyeste's daughter and his own sister. And, what is more, it turns out that this love is mutual, for Théodamie declares: *La fille de Thyeste aime le fils d'Atrée* ('Thyeste's daughter loves Atrée's son', p. 59). Thus Crébillon offers us an additional frisson: the possibility of sibling incest.

The change of locale from Argos to Euboea and the twenty-year interval are also significant. Crébillon clearly wants Thyeste to arrive in Atrée's kingdom by accident or at least against his will. Given that Argos was an inland city, such an event is most unlikely to have taken place there. Euboea, however, is an island, and Thyeste arrives as a result of shipwreck, not design. Not surprisingly, he is anxious to leave his brother's territory as soon as possible and, failing this, to keep his identity hidden. Thyeste's unwillingness even to enter his brother's realm underlines the fact that there is no political contest between the brothers and that Atrée's vengeance is purely personal. Crébillon's insistence on the twenty-year gap, and he does insist, for it is referred to three times, by Euristhène, by Théodamie and by Thyeste himself,[114] under-lines the same point. A power-hungry politician is not likely to postpone his assault for twenty years.[115]

It is not until the last scene of Act 4 that Atrée reveals Plisthène's true parentage, offering Thyeste reconciliation to be guaranteed by the return of Thyeste's son to his true father and an oath sworn by drinking from an ancestral cup. In Act 5, having sent Plisthène off for sacrifice, Atrée glories in his coming triumph in true Senecan style. At last the moment for confirming fraternal reunion arrives. Thyeste takes the cup and before drinking recognises that it contains blood. The sky darkens and Thyeste calls out for his son. The plays closes with recollections of Senecan high spots, with Thyeste declaring that he recognises his brother (*Je reconnais mon frère*, p. 92; cf. *agnosco fratrem*, *Thyestes* 1006) and with Atrée in the play's final line rejoicing in his achievements (*Et je jouis enfin du fruit de mes forfaits* ['And at last I enjoy the fruits of my crimes', p. 92]; cf. *nunc meas laudo manus, / nunc parta uera est palma* ['Now I glorify my achievements, / now the true palm is won', *Thyestes* 1096]).

For readers of Crébillon's play who are familiar with its Senecan antecedent, the most striking aspect of *Atrée et Thyeste* is its lack of horror and its lack of blood, for the brutal sacrifice and the drunken banquet are replaced by a killing which is not described and a cup which is not drained. And yet Crébillon's great dramatic rival, Voltaire, claimed that he preferred the horror of this play to Seneca's irksome declamation.[116] It seems more plausible that Voltaire could not tolerate the more explicit violence of the Senecan play, for, as Tobin observes, the myth was almost entirely ignored by French dramatists in the sixteenth, seventeenth and eighteenth centuries. Indeed, Corneille had declared the subject unsuitable for the French theatre despite the express approval of ancient critics like Aristotle and Horace.[117]

Despite his contempt for Seneca's *Thyestes*, Voltaire (1694-

1778) attempted a tragedy on the same subject. He claimed to have written the play in his youth in eleven days as a response to Crébillon's *Atrée et Thyeste*. However, in his last decade he composed a new fifth act for the play and *Les Pélopides ou Atrée et Thyeste* did not appear in print until 1771.

In the epistolary fragment which serves as preface to *Les Pélopides* ('The Descendants of Pelops') Voltaire expresses four objections to Crébillon's play. First, he disapproved of the fact that Atrée was taking revenge for an offence which had taken place twenty years earlier, arguing that such anger is only interesting and forgivable if the injury is recent. Secondly, he objected to a man planning a loathsome action in Act 1 and carrying it out in Act 5 without intrigue, obstacle or danger. Thirdly, he disliked the pointless love between Plisthène and Théodamie and, fourthly, and worst of all, he considered the play badly written.

Of the plays dealing with Atreus and Thyestes which we have considered so far it is Voltaire's which constitutes the most radically rewritten version of the myth. Certainly, it is the least dependent on Seneca's play. Voltaire sets the action at a stage earlier than other dramatists, for it takes place during the civil war between the brothers, when the relationship between Thyeste and Érope (as Voltaire calls Aerope) is still active. In addition to Atrée and Thyeste, we have their mother, Hippodamie, and Érope herself. The play takes place in the forecourt of a temple which initially serves as refuge for Hippodamie.

One primary difference between Voltaire's play and its predecessors in English and French is its overtly political character. In *Les Pélopides* Argos is caught up in civil war. Moreover, this is not simply a territory ruled by an autocrat, but a city with institutions: magistrates, senate and people. As the play begins, Polémon, who is both former tutor to Atrée and Thyeste and one of the city's archons, reveals to Hippodamie a plan to end the war provoked by Thyeste's adultery with Érope. He proposes, with the senate's support, that the estates of Pélops be shared between his sons and that Érope be restored to her husband. Only by ending their relationship can Thyeste and

Érope put a stop to civil war. Thus the play problematises the conflict between public and private, between the common good and personal desire.

However, there are obstacles to be overcome. First, as we can deduce from the play's second scene, where Érope orders Mégare to conceal *ce dépôt précieux* ('this precious deposit') in the temple, Érope and Thyeste have had a child. It becomes clear as the play progresses that the existence of the child will prove decisive for both Thyeste and Érope. Moreover, as she declares in Act 4, Érope loves both Thyeste and her son and she loathes Atrée (p. 131). Secondly, we discover in Act 3 that Atrée is not happy with the proposed treaty, for it denies him vengeance. When Idas asks *N'êtes-vous pas roi?*, Atrée replies *Non, je ne suis pas vengé* ('Are you not king? No, I am not avenged', p. 128). In the end neither party is capable of sacrificing private interests to the public good and so Atrée kills all three: the child, Érope and Thyeste. Only thus is the civil war ended.

The play's other major issue is also highlighted in Act 1: the role of destiny in this family's history. For Hippodamie in scene 1, Polémon's efforts are wasted because crime is innate in the house of Tantalus and in her own:

> The house of Tantalus had this black character: it extended to me ... In the past my father's crime was the price of my fatal/fateful love.
>
> *Les Pélopides*, p. 109

Hippodamie thus reminds us of her own father's cruelty (he killed her unsuccessful suitors) as well as that of Tantale and Pélops. By contrast, Polémon argues that *Quelquefois la sagesse a maîtrisé le sort* ('Sometimes wisdom has mastered fate'), even that *Nous faisons nos destins* ('We make our own destinies', p. 109). In her conversation with Érope in Scene 3 Hippodamie reveals her vision of the family's fate:

> In the whole of nature all arms against me: Tantalus, Pelops, my two sons and you, hell unchained and the gods in anger; every-

129

thing presents to my eyes bloody images of past misfortunes and blacker forebodings ... I see the black windings of the infernal stream, the cursed feast which Tantalus prepared, his punishment in hell ...

Les Pélopides, pp. 112, 113

It need hardly be said that it is the pessimistic Hippodamie who will be proved right. And that she was right is confirmed by Atrée's last words, the play's final speech:

Destiny, you wanted this! It is from abyss to abyss that you lead Atreus to this crowning crime ... Lightning surrounds me and the suns flees from me! Hell opens! ... I fall into eternal night. Tantalus, you come to acknowledge me your son, and my last descendants will perhaps be my equals.

Les Pélopides, p. 147

Given that Voltaire's stage-directions indicate that at this point thunder is heard and that darkness covers the earth, it seems clear that Atrée's words are to be taken literally and that he falls into hell to be welcomed by his grandfather, Tantale. Note too that his final prediction is confirmed by our knowledge of the future: Agamemnon and Menelaus will also be child-murderers. In this play destiny is inescapable.

If the full horror of *Thyestes* was too much for dramatists of the seventeenth and eighteenth centuries, it was not so in the mid-twentieth century. Hugo Claus' version, entitled *Thyestes* (1966),[118] explicitly adapted from the Senecan play, rewrites Seneca for a generation which had direct experience of maniacal and sadistic tyranny, and lived constantly with the threat of nuclear war. Claus (born 1929), a Belgian poet, novelist, dramatist and screenplay-writer, is a major figure in his own right. In a long career he has adapted a number of classical dramas including Aristophanes' *Lysistrata* (1945), Seneca's *Oedipus* (1971), Euripides' *Orestes* (1976) and Sophocles' *Oedipus at Colonus* (1986). An admirer of Antonin Artaud's theatre of cruelty, Claus completed an unfulfilled project of the master by reworking *Thyestes*.[119]

4. Reception

Although an adaptation rather than a strictly original work, Claus' *Thyestes* is the most powerful and most intriguing of the rewritings of *Thyestes*. Although adapting another's work may not seem to allow much scope for creativity, Claus finds unexpected opportunities. Consider, for example, his treatment of stage-directions. Seneca's stage-directions are of course written into the play's speeches. Claus exploits the modern convention in ways which imply a thoroughgoing engagement with the Senecan original.

The text of the play's opening consists for the most part of translation from Seneca's first act. However, the action has been reconfigured and reconceived in subtle though important ways. The setting is no longer the forecourt of Atreus' palace, but its throne room: to the left of stage is an enormous throne with the large golden skull of a ram suspended above it. The presence of the throne and the ram's skull underlines the play's focus on power. And the Fury does not drag Tantalus on stage. Rather, Tantalus comes on stage alone, with the Fury first becoming visible seated on the throne's armrest. Claus suggests not her physical power over Tantalus, but her sexual allure. We see her nakedness visible under black netting, her dazzling beauty, her thighs spread wide as she sits on the throne with Tantalus kneeling before her. Equally important is his handling of the speeches, for Claus does not treat them as merely rhetorical set pieces or as recitations. Rather, he provides detailed instructions which (of course) break up the speeches on the page, but more importantly suggest changes in tone and mood. In delivery emphasis is placed on psychological inwardness, not eloquence. In addition, Claus stages a dumb show in which Atreus sits enthroned and watches Thyestes and young Tantalus motionless before him. We see Tantalus first caressing the air around young Tantalus and then touching all three of his descendants, infecting them with his own frenzy. Although changing few words, Claus uses stage-directions not only to bring out dramatic qualities inherent in Seneca's text, but to effect significant shifts in our view of the action.

131

We see similar creative use of stage directions in the play's last scene. As Atreus enters in Seneca's Act 5, we see only Atreus until he gives instructions for the doors to be opened, when we see the drunken Thyestes. In Claus we see Thyestes from the beginning, asleep and snoring on the throne. We see him, as Atreus observes, wearing the king's robe and crown. He wakes up, he burps, he shakes his head. Even more than Seneca, Claus exploits visual means of emphasising the connection between the lust for power, on the one hand, and degradation and ignorance, on the other. Claus also brings to life important elements in the play's language. For example, he has Thyestes howling like a dog and moving about on all fours. Atreus even picks him up by the hair and pushes him towards his children's remains. It would be difficult to imagine a more effective way of underlining Atreus' mastery and the degradation of Thyestes to bestial status.

Claus' treatment of the Chorus is equally creative. Instead of the small group characteristic of the Roman stage, Claus uses one man, whom he describes as being without characteristics. Consider, for example, his first speech: it is stripped of mythological references and is addressed directly to the audience. Where the Senecan Chorus-members have some confidence in the possibility of divine assistance, Claus' Chorus, using almost the same words, has none, for he begins and ends by asking that if any god loves humanity he should speak now. The response is silence. Similarly at the end of his third speech he asks whether anyone has found the gods so kind that he is confident of being alive tomorrow. The question remains unanswered.

In so far as Claus has not reinvented Seneca's plot, his play must be classified as an adaptation. On the other hand, Claus' version represents a more thorough rethinking and certainly a more considered engagement with Seneca's text than the more original works of Crowne, Crébillon and Voltaire. For Claus, unlike his predecessors, the Thyestes myth is not just a disgusting story whose revolting details need expurgation. That he sees the play's relevance to human experience is clear from the play's closing speech. Unlike Seneca, Claus gives the last word to the Chorus, who begins thus: 'It was so. In the future it will not be otherwise.'

Notes

1. Contexts

1. For the *quinquennium Neronis* in the historiographical tradition see M.T. Griffin, *Nero: the End of a Dynasty*, pp. 37ff., 83ff.

2. Tacitus *Annals* 13.25.

3. For the significance of 62 as a turning-point see Griffin, *Nero: the End of a Dynasty*, ch. 6.

4. Tacitus *Annals* 13.3, 14.14, 15.

5. Tacitus *Annals* 15.33.

6. For details of Nero's artistic performances see Griffin, *Nero: the End of a Dynasty*, pp. 160-3.

7. The figure comes from Segala and Sciortino, *Domus Aurea*, p. 7. For detailed description and appreciation of the Domus Aurea see Macdonald, *The Architecture of the Roman Empire* I, ch. II.

8. Elder Seneca *Controuersiae* 10 pr. 4-8, Suetonius *Caligula* 16.

9. Tacitus *Annals* 1.72, 4.21.

10. Tacitus *Annals* 4.34.

11. Cassius Dio 57.22.

12. Tacitus *Annals* 6.39.

13. Tacitus *Annals* 6.29; Cassius Dio,58.24.

14. Suetonius *Caligula* 27.

15. Griffin, *Nero: the End of a Dynasty*, p. 143 speaks of a 'literary renaissance' under Nero.

16. Assuming that Calpurnius Siculus is to be assigned to Nero's reign. For a review of the arguments and a favourable evaluation of Calpurnius' achievements see Davis 'Structure and Meaning in the *Eclogues* of Calpurnius Siculus', pp. 32-54.

17. For the dates see Griffin, *Seneca: a Philosopher in Politics*, pp. 35f. This account of the first fifty years of Seneca's life is based on Griffin, ch. 2.

18. Suetonius *Caligula* 53.

19. Tacitus *Annals* 13.5.

20. Tacitus *Annals* 13.13.

21. Griffin (1976) 80f. Note Tacitus, *Annals*, 13.8 for genuine pleasure at the appointment of Corbulo, 13.46 for Otho's administrative abilities.

22. For the coinage see Griffin, *Seneca: a Philosopher in Politics*, pp.

115f. and *Nero: the End of a Dynasty*, pp. 57-9. On the absence of *maiestas* trials of senators before 62 see Griffin, *Seneca: a Philosopher in Politics*, p. 110.

23. Seneca *On Mercy* 1.1.5.

24. Tacitus *Annals* 14.7.

25. Tacitus *Annals* 14.11.

26. Tacitus *Annals* 14.52-6.

27. Tacitus *Annals* 15.45.

28. For discussion of Seneca's philosophy and its relationship with *Thyestes*, see pp. 69-74.

29. Seneca *Apocolocyntosis* 12.3.1f.

30. J.G. Fitch, 'Sense-Pauses and Relative Dating in Seneca, Sophocles and Shakespeare', pp. 289-307.

31. E.g. Tarrant , *Seneca's Thyestes*; Nisbet, 'The Dating of Seneca's Tragedies', pp. 95-114.

32. For this reason it is difficult to accept that the plays constitute a cycle (composed around 59-62), as proposed by Schubert, *Studien zum Nerobild in der lateinischen Dichtung der Antike*.

33. Tacitus *Annals* 14.26.1.

34. As Tarrant, *Seneca's Thyestes*, p. 13 n. 68; 182 suggests. Nisbet, 'The Dating of Seneca's Tragedies', pp. 104-6, supports the suggestion.

35. Coffey, 'Notes on the History of Augustan and Early Imperial Tragedy', p. 48 also favours a date early in Nero's reign.

36. Gratwick, 'Drama', p. 81.

37. See Ribbeck, *Tragicorum Romanorum Fragmenta*, pp. 364f.

38. This is the date given in Kenney and Clausen, *Cambridge History of Classical Literature 2: Latin Literature*, p. 823. However, Seneca's remark at *On Anger* 1.20.4 suggests a later date.

39. Cicero *Brutus* 78.8.

40. The fragments of this play are translated in Warmington, *Remains of Old Latin 1: Ennius and Caecilius*, pp. 346-57.

41. For this reconstruction see Jocelyn, *The Tragedies of Ennius*, p. 413.

42. The fragments of this play are translated in Warmington, *Remains of Old Latin 2: Livius Andronicus, Naevius, Pacuvius and Accius*, pp. 380-93.

43. Seneca *On Anger* 1.20.4.

2. Performance History

1. Newton, *Seneca His Tenne Tragedies*.

2. Shakespeare, *Hamlet*, Act 2, Scene 2.

3. Eliot, 'Seneca in Elizabethan Translation', p. 75.

4. Hunter, 'Shakespeare and the Traditions of Tragedy', p. 127.

5. On static elements in Senecan tragedy as evidence for unperformability see Zwierlein, *Die Rezitationsdramen Senecas*, pp. 88-126.

6. This is not to deny the effectiveness of Aeschylus' choruses: they are magnificent. However, choral odes, in so far as they do not advance the plot, can reasonably be considered a static element in a drama. With this in mind, we can say that Aeschylus' use of choral odes is one element which makes his *Agamemnon* more static than *Thyestes*. Choral odes take 295 lines of *Thyestes* in all; the first ode in Aeschylus' *Agamemnon* takes 218 lines.

7. She is called Megaera in Renaissance texts and translations.

8. Hutchinson, *Latin Literature from Seneca to Juvenal*, p. 63. See also Fitch, 'Playing Seneca?', pp. 9ff.. For discussion of how the scene might be performed, see Rosenmeyer, 'Seneca's Oedipus and Performance', p. 237, who argues that 'Manto, standing in the wings and facing outward, reports a development that is not visible to the audience'. This solution is also favoured by Hollingsworth, 'Recitational Poetry and Senecan Tragedy'.

9. Calder, 'Seneca: Tragedian of Imperial Rome', p. 4.

10. Murray, 'Verbal Play', p. 964. The play has subsequently been performed in Canada (1994) and Australia (2000). See Rutenberg, *Oedipus of Lucius Annaeus Seneca*, pp. 26-30, for an account of the production sponsored by the Department of Theatre at Hunter College, City University of New York.

11. For a discussion of the importance of what is visible in Senecan tragedy see Braun, 'La forza del visibile nelle tragedie di Seneca'. Braun discusses primarily *Hercules* (perhaps the least dramatic of the Senecan tragedies) as well as *Oedipus*, *Phaedra* and *Trojan Women*. See also Braun, 'Sind Senecas Tragödien Bühnenstücke oder Rezitationsdramen?', pp. 45f., where it is argued that the scene in which Atreus reveals the heads of Thyestes' sons is only comprehensible when performed on stage.

12. Sutton, *Seneca on the Stage*, p. 40.

13. For this see Tarrant, '*Senecan* Drama and its Antecedents', pp. 223-8; Davis, *Shifting Song*, ch. 1.

14. Zwierlein, *Die Rezitationsdramen Senecas*.

15. For a recent defence of the view that Seneca's plays were 'recitation dramas' see Mayer, *Seneca: Phaedra*, ch. 2: 'The Action of the Play'). Mayer raises a number of problems which any director of *Phaedra* must resolve.

16. Walker, 'Review of Zweierlein', p. 184.

17. Sutton, *Seneca on the Stage*.

18. Calder, 'Seneca: Tragedian of Imperial Rome'.

19. Boyle, 'Senecan Tragedy: Twelve Propositions', pp. 88f.; *Tragic Seneca*, pp. 10-12.

20. Boyle, *Seneca's Phaedra*; *Seneca's Troades*.

21. See also Kragelund, 'Senecan Tragedy: Back on Stage', who also favours stage performance, basing his case on a detailed discussion of *Phaedra* and *Octavia*.

22. Hine, *L. Annaeus Seneca: Medea*, p. 42.

23. Tarrant, *Seneca: Agamemnon*, p. 7: 'Seneca wrote with recitation, not stage-production in mind'.

24. Tarrant, *Seneca's Thyestes*, p. 122.

25. Tarrant, *Seneca's Thyestes*, p. 15 n. 77.

26. Tarrant, *Seneca's Thyestes*, p. 15.

27. Coffey and Mayer, *Seneca's Phaedra*, p. 15.

28. Harrison, *Seneca in Performance*. One of the most striking aspects of Harrison's book is the evidence it provides of a shift in the German-speaking world. See Volk, 'Putting Andromacha on Stage'. For earlier evidence of such a shift see Braun, 'La forza del visibile nelle tragedie di Seneca' and 'Sind Senecas Tragödien Bühnenstucke oder Rezitationsdramen?' and Stroh and Breitenberger, 'Inszenierung Senecas'. See also Stroh, '"Give us your applause!"'.

29. Ahl in Harrison, *Seneca in Performance*.

30. Raby in Harrison, *Seneca in Performance*.

31. Marshall in Harrison, *Seneca in Performance*.

32. Fantham in Harrison, *Seneca in Performance*, p. 13.

33. Fitch in Harrison, *Seneca in Performance*.

34. Fantham in Harrison, *Seneca in Performance*, p. 15. Fantham's claim that 'a dramatist must know when, where, and how he expects his characters to enter, take action or exit' is (presumably) true. However, dramatic texts do not always reflect that (presumed) fact. If they did, there would be no debates about this aspect of the staging of other ancient dramas. But there are. Indeed, Taplin wrote a large book, *The Stagecraft of Aeschylus*, on the subject of entrances and exits in Aeschylus, another dramatist who incorporates stage directions into the script. As Taplin, 'Did Greek Dramatists Write Stage Instructions?', p. 30, points out, ['not] every single action on the Greek stage was noticed in the words'. We might also add that even a cursory reading of the notes in modern editions of Shakespeare's plays reveals that even Shakespeare, who had the advantage of being able to use separate stage directions, did not always provide clear indication of characters' exits and entrances. In the case of both Seneca and Shakespeare this apparent deficiency in the text might well be viewed as the product of the gap between performance and publication. Moreover, the author is not the sole player here. Consideration of twentieth-century productions of *Thyestes* suggests that the way in which a play is staged is as much a decision of the director as it is of the author, for it is s/he who translates words on the page into a theatrical event.

35. *Thyestes* was performed in Dupont's translation at the Théâtre

du Lierre, Paris 75013 (5 January to 24 May 1994), at the Théâtre des
Amandiers de Nanterre (27 September to 28 October 1994), at the
Théâtre des Quartiers d'Ivry (10 October to 12 November 1995) and at
the Théâtre de Genevilliers, 92203 Genevilliers (18 November to 12
December 1999). I am grateful to Florence Dupont for this informa-
tion.

36. Dupont, *Les monstres de Sénèque*, p. 14.

37. Eliot, 'Seneca in Elizabethan Translation', p. 75.

38. Herington, 'Senecan Tragedy', p. 444.

39. Cf. *Thyestes* 257: *Sat.: ferrum? At.: parum est. Sat.: quid ignis?
At.: etiamnunc parum est* ('*Minister*: Sword? *Atreus*: Not enough.
Minister: What of fire? *Atreus*: Still not enough.')

40. Cf. F. Kermode's (*Shakespeare's Language*, p. 21) comment on
Shakespeare's use of the same device in *King John*: 'this impressive
division of one line into four speeches is surely a mark of change; the
language here is used not for elocution but for drama'.

41. Quintilian, 10.1.98; Tacitus *Annals* 11.13; Pliny *Letters* 7.17.

42. *Letters* 1.15.

43. *Moralia* 712B-D.

44. For Ovid's denial of having written for the stage, see *Tristia*
5.7.25ff. On the other hand, John Penwill points out to me that: (1)
Ovid may merely be saying that the works currently being performed
in Rome were not written for the stage, and (2) Quintilian's praise
(10.1.98) might suggest that it was. Moreover, Quintilian includes
Ovid's name in a list of tragedians who certainly did write for the
stage: Accius, Pacuvius, Varius and Pomponius Secundus.

45. For details see Van Tieghem, *La Littérature latine de la
Renaissance*, p. 147; Boas, *University Drama in the Tudor Age*, pp. 16,
18; Nelson, *Records of Early English Drama*, pp. 966ff.

46. The most valuable account of, and my most important source
for, this production is Gassman, *Tieste di Seneca*. I have also used
Marchesi, 'La prima rappresentazione del Tieste di Seneca'; Pandolfi,
'Tieste dopo duemilia anni'; and Barone, 'Gassman, Squarzina e il
Tieste di Seneca'. All claim this production as the first of the twentieth
century. See also Amoroso, 'Messa in scena di Seneca tragico',
'Spettacoli Senecani nel Ventesimo Secolo'.

47. For Squarzina's view see www.unibo.it/parol/files/squarzina.htm.
According to Esslin, *Artaud*, p. 37, Artaud had planned a production of
Thyestes: 'In 1932 he was busy on an adaptation of Seneca's tragedy of
Atreus and Thyestes'.

48. Gassman, *Tieste di Seneca*, p. 90.

49. Marchesi, 'La prima rappresentazione del Tieste di Seneca', p. 47.

50. Marchesi, 'La prima rappresentazione del Tieste di Seneca', p. 45.

51. Marchesi, 'La prima rappresentazione del Tieste di Seneca', pp.
45, 46); Pandolfi, 'Tieste dopo duemilia anni', pp. 45, 46.

52. This account is based on Small, 'Atrocity in a Fog', and Bruce, 'Glasgow: Seneca's *Thyestes*'.

53. Watling, *Seneca: Four Tragedies and Octavia*.

54. This seems to have been the only US production of the play. The Billy Rose Theatre Collection at the Lincoln Center for the Performing Arts in New York has no record of any production of *Thyestes* in the USA (including this one). The Harvard Theatre Collection has records only for this production. I am grateful to the librarians at both institutions.

55. This description is based on the original programme notes held in the Archive for Performances of Greek and Roman Drama at Oxford. The quotations come from Agapitos' own account, 'Staging *Thyestes*'.

56. In 1990, Michael Hurst, a distinguished New Zealand actor and director, perhaps best known for his role in the television series *Xena: Warrior Princess,* directed *Thyestes* as part of a trilogy entitled *The House of Atreus*, consisting of *Thyestes* (Part 1), Euripides' *Iphigenia in Aulis* and Aeschylus' *Agamemnon* (Part 2) and Euripides' *Electra* and *Orestes* (Part 3) at the Auckland Performing Arts School. In order to bring out the idea of a curse spanning generations, Hurst used actors belonging to different age groups for each of the three parts of his trilogy, teenagers for *Thyestes*, 20- to 40-year-olds for *Agamemnon* and *Iphigenia* and 50- and 60-year-olds for *Electra* and *Orestes*. The production was, it seems, a great success, with a cast of 60 teenagers revelling in Seneca's blood and rhetoric. Hurst emphasised the play's ritualistic nature and epic theatricality. I have included this production in a footnote rather than in the text because, given that the whole performance took two and a half hours, the *Thyestes* section of the trilogy must have been a much abbreviated version of the play. I would like to thank Michael Hurst for this information.

57. This account is based on Raboni, 'Un "Tieste" di solo donne che pare uscito da uno spot'.

58. There was another production in Italy in the 1990s: in March and April 1998 at the Teatro dell'Angelo in Rome, using a Mafia setting and Sicilian dialect. I have not been able to obtain much detail concerning this production. But see Audino, 'Seneca e Plauto fra i dilaletti'; D'Amico, 'Tieste ovvero la vendetta mafiosa'.

59. I would like to thank Professor Filippo Amoroso of the University of Palermo for providing me with a videotape of this production. My account is based on this tape.

60. My account of the use of video is based primarily on Coveney, 'Seneca's *Thyestes*'; Keen, 'Review: Lucius Annaeus Seneca's *Thyestes*'; Taylor, 'Viler than Violence'.

61. Taylor, 'Viler than Violence'.

62. Eliot, 'Seneca in Elizabethan Translation', p. 68.

63. Gross, 'A full-bodied, bloody wine'.

64. Wardle, 'The Greeks had words for it; we don't'.

65. Hall, 'Things Go Badly'.

66. Keen, 'Review; Lucius Annaeus Seneca's *Thyestes*'.

67. Coveney, 'Seneca's *Thyestes*'.

68. Taylor, 'Viler than Violence'.

69. Gross, 'A full-bodied, bloody wine'; Wardle, 'The Greeks had words for it; we don't'.

70. Roger Blin had planned to stage what would have been the first twentieth-century French production of *Thyestes* in Paris in 1968. Aslan, *Roger Blin and Twentieth Century Playwrights*, p. 114, reports that 'Blin wanted to direct the play [Robert Weingarten's *The Carrion-Eaters*] in Paris in the autumn, but he was prevented by the events of 1968, which also prevented his staging Seneca's *Thyestes*, a play that tempted Artaud'. Peter Brook's claim ('Peter Brook Talking to Frank Cox about Seneca's *Oedipus*') that Blin actually did produce *Thyestes* seems to be mistaken. *Thyestes* is not listed in Peskine's catalogue of productions.

71. My account of this production is based on Salino, 'Les monstres de Seneque ne font pas du quartier'; Schmitt, 'Thyeste à Nanterre-Amandiers'; Mayrhofer, 'The Complete Plays of Seneca'.

72. Salino, 'Les monstres de Seneque ne font pas du quartier'.

73. Dupont, *L'Acteur-roi*, p. 451.

74. Cournot, 'Un Sénèque un peu anachronique et qui vous étourdit de beauté'.

3. Themes and Issues

1. This essay was first published in 1927.

2. E.g. Herington ('Senecan Tragedy', p. 458) rates *Thyestes*, along with *Phaedra*, as 'the finest in the Senecan corpus'. Braden ('The Rhetoric and Psychology of Power in the Dramas of Seneca', p. 29) speaks of *Medea* and *Thyestes* as 'probably Seneca's best realized plays'. Calder ('Seneca: Tragedian of Imperial Rome', p. 7) calls *Thyestes* 'Seneca's greatest tragedy'. Motto and Clark ('Senecan Tragedy', p. 363) declare *Thyestes* 'Seneca's most powerful drama'. Seidensticker and Armstrong ('Seneca Tragicus 1878-1978', p. 922) view *Thyestes* as 'the masterpiece of the group'. Tarrant (*Seneca's Thyestes*, p. 43) sees *Thyestes* as 'an extraordinarily cohesive play, in which all the elements of drama – plot, character, setting, language – work together to produce an impact of shattering power'.

3. As Herington ('Senecan Tragedy', p. 427) points out, 'this mistake of Eliot's may, in fact, be classified as a Freudian slip: even in a passage when he is, quite rightly protesting against the widespread belief that Senecan drama is simply crammed with horrors, he still cannot shake off the even more widely spread ancestral opinion that at any rate it ought to be gorier than *Greek* drama'.

4. Nauck (*TGrF*) lists an *Aerope* by Agathon and Carcinus, an *Atreus* by Sophocles, and a *Thyestes* by Agathon, Apollodorus, Carcinus, Chaeremon, Cleophon, Diogenes, Euripides and Sophocles. It is possible that Sophocles wrote three plays on Thyestes. See Lloyd-Jones, *Sophocles: Fragments*, p. 106ff.

5. Many ancient plays, especially by Euripides, begin with a prologue delivered by a single divine speaker who does not reappear. More rare is the use of two divinities (Euripides' *Trojan Women* and *Alcestis* are examples). A closer parallel is Euripides' treatment of Iris and Lyssa in the body (not the prologue) of *Heracles*, with Iris, like the Fury, inciting the unwilling Lyssa. See Monteleone, 'I modelli di Seneca nel prologo del *Thyestes*', p. 79; G. Picone, *La Fabula e il Regno*, p. 16. The use of a ghostly prologue is rare (Euripides employs the device in *Hecuba*, Seneca in *Agamemnon*, with the important difference that Polydorus is Hecuba's descendant, while Thyestes is Aegisthus' ancestor). *Thyestes* is unique in combining ghostly ancestor (Tantalus) with divinity (the Fury).

6. She is labelled *Furia* in E, *Megaera* in A. Modern editors follow E.

7. The story is told at *Metamorphoses* 6.411-674.

8. E.g. Euripides *Electra* 727-36, *Iphigenia in Tauris* 816, *Orestes* 1001-6; Plato *Statesman* 268E-269A all present sun's reversal of its course as part of the Atreus-Thyestes myth, though not a response to the banquet.

9. The idea of *alternum scelus* ('alternating crime') is also prominent in *Agamemnon* (44, 65, 77).

10. As Boyle (*Tragic Seneca*, p. 44) points out: 'It not only predicts the horror to come ..., but its structure (resistance to hunger/*furor*, followed by subservience to hunger/*furor*) and even its formula for submission ('I follow', *sequor*, 100, 489) prove models for the dramatic and tragic turning point: Thyestes' capitulation to the new Tantalus'. Schiesaro's argument ('Seneca's *Thyestes* and the Morality of Tragic *furor*', pp. 197, 198, 203) that '*Thyestes* begins by staging the process of its own construction', that 'this prefatory debate is a symbolic enactment of the birth of the play' and that 'the debate between the Fury and Tantalus actually illuminates the genesis of the play' points to Seneca being concerned with the relationship between playwright and play, with the idea that 'to sing of *nefas* is, in a sense, to perpetrate it' (202). To make this case Schiesaro needs to point to explicitly theatrical language in Act 1. He does not. It is much easier to discern meta-dramatic elements in Acts 3 and 5 where Thyestes unwittingly enacts the script of playwright Atreus, as Schiesaro realises (p. 196), and in Act 4 where the messenger seems carried away by his own performance and by the internal audience's (i.e. the Chorus's) response.

11. For this see Steidle, 'Die Gestalt des Thyest', pp. 497f., and Hine, 'The Structure of Seneca's *Thyestes*', p. 267.

12. For this point see Calder, 'Seneca *Thyestes* 101-106'.

13. E.g. Gigon, 'Bemerkungen zu Senecas *Thyestes*'; Herington, 'Senecan Tragedy'; Poe, 'An Analysis of Seneca's *Thyestes*'; La Penna, 'Atreo e Tieste sulle scene Romane'. Hine ('The Structure of Seneca's *Thyestes*', p. 273) considers him 'a *prokoptôn*, someone advancing on the road of moral improvement'.

14. As Boyle, *Tragic Seneca*, p. 49, points out: 'The "persuasion" scene is conspicuous for its absence of persuasiveness.'

15. Older texts, following A, labelled this son Plisthenes. All modern texts, following E, are agreed in calling him 'Tantalus'.

16. Cf. Seneca *On Mercy* 1.19.2.

17. For this point see Tarrant, *Seneca's Thyestes*, p. 149.

18. The point is well made by Tarrant, *Seneca's Thyestes*, p. 158: 'This attempt at a ringing *sententia* falls short of conviction. The choice of *pati* is revealing, a sort of "Freudian slip": by saying that he can "manage" or "get along" without a kingdom Thyestes shows that he ... regards power as a positive good.' Much better than Heywood and Watling is Caryl Churchill's translation (*Lucius Annaeus Seneca: Thyestes*, p. 19): 'You have vast power if you / can manage without power.'

19. Hence I agree with Boyle's evaluation of Thyestes (*Tragic Seneca*, p. 51): 'he is deluded by a world he castigated as deluding ... Hunger triumphs in Thyestes as it does in Atreus; and disgust'. See also Tarrant, *Seneca's Thyestes*, pp. 148f.

20. For this see Boyle, *Tragic Seneca*, p. 53.

21. For this see Boyle, *Tragic Seneca*, p. 47.

22. Boyle, *Tragic Seneca*, p. 46. On this aspect of *Thyestes* see also Dupont, *Les monstres de Sénèque*, pp. 193-6.

23. Cf. Boyle, *Tragic Seneca*, pp. 54, 56.

24. For the shifts of meaning of *modus* see Tarrant, *Seneca's Thyestes*, p. 236.

25. For a more detailed account of the choruses in *Thyestes* see Davis, 'The Chorus in Seneca's *Thyestes*'. For the choruses in Senecan tragedy generally see Davis, *Shifting Song*.

26. Cf. the Stoic notion that only the wise man is truly king, e.g. Cicero *Pro Murena* 61.

27. For self-sufficiency see Seneca *Epistles* 9.3-5, 12-19; for looking down on human affairs see *Epistles* 73.14 (where the wise man is compared to Jupiter); cf. Cicero *Tusculan Disputations* 3.15.

28. Nero is addressed as being 18 years old (1.9.1). Since he was born on 15 December 37, *On Mercy* must have been published between December 55 and December 56.

29. See Griffin, *Seneca: A Philosopher in Politics*, p. 204.

30. This connection is also noted by Mader, '*Quod nolunt velint*', p. 37.

31. This point is made by Tarrant, *Seneca's Thyestes*, p. 121.

32. Calder, 'Seneca: Tragedian of Imperial Rome', pp. 8f.

33. As Mader, '*Quod nolunt velint*', p. 41, points out, 'the satellite's insistence on his *fides* is an overt act of flattery which corresponds exactly to the "praise on demand" required by the tyrant (206f.)'. We might compare Tacitus' comment (*Annals* 14.56.14) on the conclusion of another minister's interview with his master: *Seneca, qui finis omnium cum dominante sermonum, grates agit* ('Seneca, this is the end of every conversation with a tyrant, gave thanks').

34. As is clear from *On Anger*, the fact that Seneca speaks of such cruelty as 'madness' does not mean that he regards a character like Atreus as free of moral responsibility. At *On Anger* 2.3.5 he explains that anger (and anger is characteristic of Atreus) is the 'excitement of a mind moving towards revenge by choice and judgement'. Anger is also said to be a 'brief madness' (1.2.2), while *feritas* ('bestial cruelty') is said to arise from habitual indulgence in anger (2.5.3). Both are plainly culpable.

35. Poe, 'An Analysis of Seneca's *Thyestes*', p. 359.

36. Poe, 'An Analysis of Seneca's *Thyestes*', p. 355.

37. See Davis, '*Vindicat omnes natura sibi*', and Boyle, *Tragic Seneca*, pp. 60-7.

38. See Motto and Clark, 'Seneca's *Thyestes* as Melodrama'.

39. As Calder, '*Secreti Loquimur*', p. 186, points out.

40. Aristotle *Poetics* 1449a18.

41. 707, 379.

42. 354-7.

43. 370, 384, 462, 602f., 629f.

44. 24, 52, 264, 775.

45. 396.

46. The description of the Argive royal palace at 641ff., as Tarrant, *Seneca's Thyestes*, p. 183, points out, alludes to Virgil's account of Latinus' dwelling (*Aeneid* 7.170-91), which itself refers to Augustus' dwelling on the Palatine. Seneca's description may, however, refer to Nero's extension of his residence from the Palatine towards the Esquiline (the Domus Transitoria) (Suetonius *Nero* 31.1.).

4. Reception

1. See Tarrant, *Seneca's Thyestes*, p. 134.

2. See Lebek, 'Seneca's Agamemnon in Pompeji'.

3. *Octavia* survived along with genuinely Senecan tragedies only in the A-branch of the manuscript tradition. Although some scholars still believe the play to be by Seneca, most do not. In my view, the most persuasive reason for not accepting Senecan authorship is that the play seems to foreshadow events which took place after Seneca's death, in particular, the revolt of Vindex (255f.) and the squalid circumstances of Nero's death (619-31). The fact that Seneca is a character in the play also makes it unlikely that he is its author.

4. For example, the author follows Greek precedent in giving the final lines to the Chorus. Also its action clearly takes place over more than one day. (However, this may be characteristic of the *praetexta* rather than a sign of non-Senecan authorship.) Some unusual features (use of the double Chorus and six-act structure) have parallels in genuine works.

5. Compare also the Nurse's denial of Love's divinity (*Phaedra* 195ff.) with Seneca's similar denial (*Octavia* 557ff.).

6. Calder, '*Secreti Loquimur*', p. 193, points out that *Octavia* is 'our earliest commentary on *Thyestes*'.

7. The connection has been noted before. Vessey, *Statius and the Thebaid*, p. 77: 'There are analogies too in the *Thyestes*. In that drama, two brothers, cursed by their father and members of a *devota domus*, claim the same throne and meditate mutual vengeance.'

8. *Thebaid* 6. 280, 284.

9. *Thebaid* 1.325, 2.184, 3.308-10, 11.127-9.

10. *Thebaid* 11.127f.

11. *Thebaid* 8.742.

12. Henderson, 'Statius' *Thebaid*/Form premade', p. 52. See also Vessey, *Statius and the Thebaid*, pp. 72-8, and Feeney, *The Gods in Epic*, pp. 347f.

13. Vessey, *Statius and the Thebaid*, p. 7.

14. The classic statement of the case for Senecan influence on Elizabethan tragedy in general is Cunliffe, *The Influence of Seneca on Elizabethan Tragedy*. Significant criticism of Cunliffe's approach is to be found in Hunter, 'Seneca and the Elizabethans'. For a more careful and more convincing statement of the case for Senecan influence see Daalder, *Lucius Annaeus Seneca/Jasper Heywood: 'Thyestes'*, pp. xx-xxvii; Boyle, *Tragic Seneca*.

15. For convenience I have adopted the dates given in the chronological table in Braunmuller and Hattaway, *Cambridge Companion to English Renaissance Drama*. Some of these dates are controversial.

16. See Reynolds, *Texts and Transmission*, p. 360.

17. The figures come from Smith, 'Seneca's Tragedies'.

18. The play is called *Troas* ('The Trojan Woman' or possibly even 'The Troad') in the A-branch of the manuscript tradition. It is called *Troades* ('Trojan Women') in the Codex Etruscus (E).

19. See Smith, 'Seneca's Tragedies' , pp. 69f.). For discussion of Heywood's translation see Daalder, *Lucius Annaeus Seneca/Jasper Heywood: 'Thyestes'*.

20. Newton, *Seneca His Tenne Tragedies*.

21. Both are referred to in the preface to Heywood's translation:

'There Sackville's Sonnets sweetly sauc'd and featly fined be; / There Norton's ditties do delight ...' (91f).

22. Quoted by Baker, *Induction to Tragedy*, p. 10) and Herrick, 'Senecan Influence in *Gorboduc*', p. 78. The pro-Senecan position is set out by Cunliffe, *The Influence of Seneca on Elizabethan Tragedy*, and Charlton, *The Senecan Tradition in Renaissance Tragedy*.

23. Baker, *Induction to Tragedy*, pp. 37f.

24. Baker, *Induction to Tragedy*, p. 38.

25. E.g. Horace *Art of Poetry* 189.

26. *Gorboduc* 3.1.16. For the text of *Gorboduc* I have used McIlwraith, *Five Elizabethan Tragedies*. Cf. *Trojan Women* 145.

27. *Gorboduc* Chorus 3.1.

28. McIlwraith, *Five Elizabethan Tragedies*, p. 88, suggests that the third victim is Prometheus. However, in the light of *Thyestes* 5-12, lines spoken by Tantalus which include references to Ixion and Tityos, it seems more likely that Tityos is being referred to. See also *Agamemnon* 12-21, lines which allude to Ixion, Tityos and Tantalus.

29. Though Act 5, Scene 3 of *Agamemnon* involves four speakers: Clytemnestra, Electra, Aegisthus and Cassandra. Some alleged unclassical features, absence of a single central character and changes of scene, can be paralleled in Seneca. Seneca's *Agamemnon* and *Trojan Women* both lack a central character and changes of scene seem likely within Act 2 and between Acts 3 and 5 of *Trojan Women*. Unity of time (not found in *Gorboduc*) is observed in the genuine Senecan tragedies, but not in *Octavia*, then regarded as Senecan.

30. Watson, 'Tragedy', p. 318.

31. For the text of *The Spanish Tragedy* I have used Mulryne, *Thomas Kyd: The Spanish Tragedy*. 'Horn' is a plainly correct emendation of 'Horror'. Smith, *Thomas Kyd: The Spanish Tragedie*, retains 'Horror' and so robs the text of significant point.

32. The similarity between the openings of *Thyestes* and *The Spanish Tragedy* was noted by Boas, *The Works of Thomas Kyd*, p. 393. Baker's (*Induction to Tragedy*, pp. 108f.) objection that the use of the ghost and Revenge is purely medieval is mistaken. First, it should be noted that 'Senecan' and 'medieval' are not mutually exclusive terms. It is more accurate to say that Kyd creatively exploits two traditions, one native, one classical. Secondly, it is not true that personifications like Revenge are 'exclusively medieval', for personifications are common in Roman literature (e.g. Rumour in *Aeneid* 4, Sleep in *Metamorphoses* 11, Piety and Virtue in *Thebaid* 10, Faith in *Punica* 2) and, even though they have individual names, Furies are effectively personifications. Moreover, personifications are common in Roman art and standard on Roman coins. Bowers' (*Elizabethan Revenge Tragedy*, p. 66) comparison of Andrea with Achilles in *Trojan Women* is odd since Achilles does not appear on stage (though he does in Heywood's translation) and it is not the case that Achilles seeks revenge for death in battle.

33. P. Mercer, *'Hamlet' and the Acting of Revenge*, p. 15. See also Hill, 'Senecan and Vergilian Perspectives in The Spanish Tragedy', pp. 144ff.

34. 1.3.15, quoting *Doctrinale Minus alias Liber Parabolarum* 2.18 (Migne, vol. 210, column 584),

35. 1.2.12-13, adapting *de tertio consulatu Honorii* 96-8.

36. 2.5.71, *in luminis oras* is used four times by Lucretius. It is also possible that the phrase derives from *Georgics* 2.47, a work with many Lucretian reminiscences.

37. 2.5.67, recalling *Metamorphoses* 15.97; 2.5.69 recalling *ex Ponto* 4.10.19; 2.5.74 quoting *Heroides* 20.83.

38. 1.2.55f., quoting *Thebaid* 8.389f. (or possibly Virgil or Ovid or Silius Italicus); 2.5.68, quoting *Siluae* 5.1.16.

39. 2.5.70, quoting 2.2.13.

40. *scriptum est enim mihi uindictam ego retribuam dicit Dominus* ('For it is written: "Vengeance is mine; I will repay, says the Lord" '). Daalder, 'The Role of "Senex" in Kyd's *The Spanish Tragedy*', p. 253, among others, sees a reference to Nero's words at *Octavia* 849. Hieronimo's reflections on the quotation make this unlikely. Braden, *Renaissance Tragedy and the Senecan Tradition*, p. 202, sees a reference to both texts.

41. Hence I agree with the view of Ratliff, 'Hieronimo Explains Himself', p. 117: 'Clytemnestra's example is a warning that a criminal may seek safety by killing anyone who could threaten him – that he may seek to forestall revenge'. Unfortunately Ratliff does not discuss the quotations from *Trojan Women* or *Oedipus*.

42. Although the lines are slightly rearranged, the words are quoted in the correct order and with absolute precision – not loosely, as Smith, *Thomas Kyd: The Spanish Tragedie*, p. 173, claims. Indeed it is her text which is loose, for she prints the second *Fata* as Futa, which is meaningless. Worse is the Latin in 2.5 (her p. 32) which contains at least fourteen errors in fourteen lines.

43. For the text of *Titus Andronicus* I have used Bate, *William Shakespeare: Titus Andronicus*. The best study of Shakespeare's use of *Thyestes* is Miola, *Shakespeare and Classical Tragedy*, pp. 13-32. Because this study is so fine and so comprehensive I have tried to concentrate on an aspect of the relationship between the two plays upon which Miola barely touches.

44. Baker, *Induction to Tragedy*, p. 122: 'this is what connects *Andronicus* with Ovid and probably with Ovid alone'. Baker is willing to allow that there is one resemblance between *Thyestes* and *Titus Andronicus*: the number of victims cooked. In this he is mistaken, for Titus and Lavinia cook two sons of Tamora (Chiron and

Demetrius), while Atreus cooks three sons of Thyestes (Tantalus 717f., Plisthenes 726, and an unnamed son 740; see also 1023: *fruere, osculare, diuide amplexus tribus* 'enjoy them, kiss them, divide your embraces among the three'). It is particularly significant that both recent editors of the play – Waith, *Shakespeare: Titus Andronicus*, p. 37; and Bate, *Shakespeare and Ovid*, p. 103 n. 33, and *William Shakespeare: Titus Andronicus*, p. 29 n. 2 – endorse Baker's view. So too does Goldberg, 'Going for Baroque', p. 217. The principal exceptions to this generalisation are the masterly studies of Daalder, *Lucius Annaeus Senaeca / Jasper Heywood: 'Thyestes'*, pp. xxvii-xxxi), Miola, *Shakespeare and Classical Tragedy*, and Boyle, *Tragic Seneca*.

45. For the importance of Plutarch's *Life of Scipio Africanus* see Law, 'The Roman Background of *Titus Andronicus*', p. 147.

46. At 4.2.21f. Demetrius reads out the first two lines of *Odes* 1.22; at 1.1.633 Demetrius seems to quote *Odes* 1.18.10-11. Titus (5.3.36f.) refers to the story of Appius and Verginia (Livy 3.44).

47. For an excellent discussion of Shakespeare's use of Virgil see James, *Shakespeare's Troy*, ch. 2.

48. For both events the occasion is a hunt; like Dido, Lavinia is compared to a doe (1.1.617, 2.1.26; cf. *Aeneid* 4.68-73); and in both cases Fame (i.e. Rumour) is mentioned. Aaron refers to the house of Fame (1.1.626), a clear allusion to Ovid *Metamorphoses* 12.39-63. In the context, however, we should also be reminded of Virgil *Aeneid* 4.173-88. For the importance of Lavinia's name and her resemblances to Virgil's Lavinia see Law, 'The Roman Background of *Titus Andronicus*', p. 146.

49. Both Dido and Tamora are likened to Diana (*Aeneid* 1.498-504; *Titus* 1.1.320ff., 2.2.57); Tamora herself invokes the analogy (2.2.22-4). Note that Tamora and Aaron might even be seen as a racial inversion of Virgil's lovers, for she is quasi-Roman while he is African.

50. Miola, '*Titus Andronicus* and the Mythos of Shakespeare's Rome', p. 89. For the fall of Troy see 3.2.27f., 5.3.79-86. Miola also points to the importance of *Eclogue* 4.

51. 1.1.139ff., 4.1.20; cf. *Metamorphoses* 13.429ff.

52. 1.1.384ff.; cf. *Metamorphoses* 13.382-98.

53. 1.1.608, 3.1.299, 4.1.63f., 4.1.91; cf. *Fasti*, 2.685-852. Livy 1.57-8 is also an important source for this story.

54. 1.6.26; cf. *Metamorphoses* 12.39-63.

55. 2.2.61-5; cf. *Metamorphoses* 3.155-252.

56. 2.2.231; cf. *Metamorphoses* 4.55-166.

57. 2.3.51; cf. *Metamorphoses* 10.1-85, 11.1-66. The story is also familiar from Virgil, *Georgics* 4.

58. Lavinia's mode of communication with Titus and Marcus in 4.1 recalls Io's revelation of her identity in *Metamorphoses* 1.649f.

59. At 4.3.4 Titus quotes in Latin *Metamorphoses* 1.150: *terras Astraea reliquit* ('Astraea left the earth'), Astraea's departure marking the end of the golden age (cf. Virgil *Eclogue* 4.6).

60. 5.2.203; cf. *Metamorphoses* 12.210-535.

61. See also 2.2.43, 2.3.26ff., 5.2.194f.

62. As will become apparent, I reject Hunter's ('Seneca and the Elizabethans', p. 22) claim that 'the Senecan quotations which appear in Elizabethan plays, even when the quantity is as great as that which decorates Marston's *Antonio and Mellida*, bear little or no relation to the contexts in which they originally appeared'. This is not true of Shakespeare and it is not true of Marston.

63. The Fury also sees Tereus and/or Procne as a model, for she longs for a Thracian crime (*Thracium fiat nefas*, 56).

64. The ancients identified the planets and other heavenly bodies with gods (hence of course their names in English).

65. This connection was first noted by Law, 'The Roman Background of *Titus Andronicus*'. It was subsequently denied by Hansen, 'Two Notes on Seneca and *Titus Andronicus*'. It has been reasserted and discussed in detail by De Armas, 'Astraea's Fall'. See also the detailed discussion in Sutherland, 'Shakespeare and Seneca', pp. 134-7. Miola, *Shakespeare and Classical Tragedy*, p. 32, is aware of the connection but does not pursue it.

66. De Armas, 'Astraea's Fall', p. 306.

67. Miola, *Shakespeare and Classical Tragedy*, p. 23.

68. Boyle, *Tragic Seneca*, p. 46.

69. Hamilton, *The Early Shakespeare*, pp. 74f.

70. Note especially *Thyestes* 627-32.

71. *Octavia* 453: Nero's maxim *inertis est nescire quid liceat sibi* ('it is the mark of a sluggish man not to know what he can do') is translated as by Piero as "Tis horse-like not for man to know his force' (1.1.86). Because sixteenth- and seventeenth-century scholars and dramatists included *Octavia* in the Senecan corpus, I will do likewise for the purposes of this discussion.

72. Rosaline ('Pish, 'tis our nature to desire things / That are thought strangers to the common cut', 1.1.146f.) quotes Phaedra's Nurse (204f.). 4.1.292 recalls *Phaedra* 607.

73. Antonio's description of the storm (1.1.212ff.) recalls details from the storm narrative in *Agamemnon*, especially lines 463 (cf. 1.1.212), 468 (cf. 1.1.215), 499f. (cf. 1.1.221f.).

74. Andrugio's assertion of survival (3.1.59f.) recalls Medea's famous claim *Medea superest* (166, 'Medea remains'), while his next two lines recall the end of Medea's exchange with the Nurse in the same scene (176). The exchange between Andrugio and Lucio at 4.1.296-299 translates and then quotes in Latin *Medea* 159-61.

75. Lucio's comment 'Of all your forces and your utmost hopes: / A

149

weak old man, a page and your poor self' (3.1.83f.) recalls *Trojan Women* 507f.

76. 3.2.51f. recalls *Oedipus* 705f.

77. 3.2.194 translates *Phoenician Women* 152f.

78. Andrugio quotes *Hercules Oetaeus* 756 (*O lares, miseri lares!*) at 4.1.86.

79. Finkelpearl, *John Marston of the Middle Temple*, p. 149.

80. For the text of Marston's plays I have used Sturgess, *John Marston*.

81. As Hunter, 'Ironies of Justice in The Spanish Tragedy', p. xiv, points out: 'Similarly Marston places Andrugio's noble description of the true prince (IV.i.46ff.) immediately before an exchange in which the pose of *apatheia* is betrayed into passionate involvement'. See also Berland, 'The Function of Irony in Marston's *Antonio and Mellida*'.

82. As Hunter, 'Ironies of Justice in *The Spanish Tragedy*', p. xiv, observes: 'Marston immediately follows this paean by a scene in which the fine sentiments are undercut by Feliche's patent inability to support them'. Berland, 'The Function of Irony in Marston's *Antonio and Mellida*', p. 751, points out that 'He is as guilty of self-deception as the courtiers and the rulers he excoriates'.

83. For the similarities in structure between the two plays see Hunter, *John Marston: Antonio's Revenge*, p. x.

84. 1.2.334-5 translates Seneca *Dialogues* 1.1.6.

85. Cf. Seneca *Medea* 155f.: *leuis est dolor, qui capere consilium potest / et clepere sese: magna non latitant mala.*

86. *Octavia* 632: *heu, quo labor, quo uota ceciderunt mea?*

87. Hunter, *John Marston: Antonio's Revenge*, p. xvii, speaks of 'Antonio's Black Requiem', pointing out that 'the censing and asperging (with the blood of his enemy) the tomb of his own father seems to be a direct reference to the Requiem Mass'.

88. He quotes *Agamemnon* 154: *capienda rebus in malis praeceps uia est.* Modern texts print *rapienda*, not *capienda*, following E, a manuscript not available to Renaissance editors.

89. The cutting out of the tongue was presumably inspired by Tereus' treatment of Philomela in Ovid (*Metamorphoses* 6.555ff.) and/or by Hieronimo's biting out of his own tongue in *The Spanish Tragedy*.

90. As Boyle, *Tragic Seneca*, p. 146, points out. As far as I am aware, Boyle is the first to realise the importance of *Thyestes* as an intertext for the *Antonio* plays.

91. For the text of *Sejanus* I have used Ayres, *Ben Jonson: Sejanus His Fall*.

92. As Barton, *Ben Jonson, Dramatist*, p. 97, observes, 'What in Seneca was grand has become distinctly ridiculous.'

93. For the text of *Catiline* I have used Bolton and Gardner, *Ben Jonson, Catiline*.

94. As Barton, *Ben Jonson, Dramatist*, p. 165, points out.

95. Hence I find Barton's (*Ben Jonson, Dramatist*, p. 156) reference to the 'over-blown Senecan world of the conspirators' puzzling.

96. The choice of Sulla is presumably prompted by Sallust's suggestion that he was Catiline's model (Sallust *Catiline* 5.6).

97. For the importance of Senecan tragedy in Italy and France see Boyle, *Tragic Seneca*, chs 7, 8 and 9 *passim*). Boyle discusses Cinzio but not Garnier.

98. For the text of *Orbecche* I have used Ariani, *Il teatro italiano*. I have also adopted his spelling of the author's name.

99. For discussion of *Orbecche's* relationship with *Thyestes* see Horne, *The Tragedies of Giambattista Cinthio Giraldi*, ch. 3; Boyle, *Tragic Seneca*; and Morrison, *The Tragedies of G.-B. Giraldi Cinthio*.

100. Note the reference to Hyrcania at *Thyestes* 631 and *Orbecche* 4.1.2.

101. For the text of *Les Juifves* I have used Lebègue, *Robert Garnier: Les Juifves* etc.

102. Lebègue, *Robert Garnier: Les Juifves*, p. 14. In the Loeb edition of *Jewish Antiquities* the relevant passage is Book 10.138-41. Garnier's citation of sources is problematical. See, for example, DiMauro, 'Garnier's Historical Sources in *Les Juifves*', pp. 21-31.

103. That Garnier knew and exploited Senecan tragedy is not controversial. His *Hippolyte*, for example, contains long passages directly translated from Seneca's *Phaedra*. For discussion see Davis, 'Rewriting Seneca: Garnier's *Hippolyte*'.

104. Mueller, *Children of Oedipus*, p. 179, points out that Euripides' *Hecuba* is also an important intertext, because the fate of Polymestor foreshadows that of Sédécie.

105. Wright is alleged to be a barrister by Maidment and Logan, *The Dramatic Works of John Crowne*, p. 9: 'Of Wright we have no further account than that he was a barrister.'

106. For the text of *Mock Thyestes* I have used Wright, *Thyestes, A Tragedy*.

107. The translation is not of special interest. Certainly it does not reflect the fact that knowledge of the text of Seneca's tragedies had been revolutionised by the publication of Gronovius' edition in 1661.

108. For the text of Crowne's *Thyestes* I have used Maidment and Logan, *The Dramatic Works of John Crowne*. Halliwell, *A Dictionary of Old English Plays*, p. 246, notes that 'it is the only piece on this story that has made its appearance on the English stage, where it met with good success'.

109. Crowne and the king seem to have been on good terms. We are told, for example, that when Crowne was suffering playwright's block the king suggested to him the plot which became one of Crowne's great successes, *Sir Courtly Nice or It Cannot Be*. See Fraser, *King Charles*

II, p. 298. More significantly, his comedy *City Politiques* (January 1683) satirises the king's prime opponents, the Whigs. For the politics of this play see Wilson, *John Crowne: City Politiques*, pp. xi-xix. White, *John Crowne*, p. 40, characterises Crowne as 'an ardent Tory'.

110. See Smith, *Ancient Scripts and Modern Experience on the English Stage*, pp. 259ff.

111. Crowne was Anglican in religion but more hostile to Catholicism than many dissenters. White, *John Crowne*, pp. 53ff., notes that anti-Catholic outbursts are common in Crowne's plays. He argues that passages in *Thyestes* are reminiscent of 'the rabid anti-Jesuit pamphlets of the day' (p. 55).

112. For the text of Crébillon's *Atrée et Thyeste* I have used Vitu, *J. De Crébillon: Théâtre Complet*. For the play's reception see Dunkley, *Prosper Jolyot de Crébillon: Electre*. Tobin, 'Nourriture, bienséances et tragédie', notes two earlier French plays on Thyestes by Roland Brisset (1589) and Monléon (1638). I have not seen these plays. There is a discussion of Monléon's *Thyeste* in Lancaster, *A History of French Dramatic Literature in the Seventeen Century*, part II, pp. 156f.

113. For detailed discussion of Senecan allusions in Crébillon and Voltaire see Rossi, *Una metafora presa alla lettera*, ch. 3.

114. Vitu, *J. De Crébillon: Théâtre Complet*, pp. 51, 58, 69.

115. Of course the twenty-year gap is also necessary so that Plisthène can be an adult.

116. For the text of Voltaire I have used Moland, *Oeuvres Complètes de Voltaire*.

117. Tobin, 'Nourriture, bienséances et tragédie', p. 177 n. 18; Aristotle *Poetics* 1453a21; Horace *Ars Poetica* 91, 186.

118. Since I do not read Flemish, I have used two French translations as the basis of this discussion: Claus, *Thyeste*, trans. Maddy Buysse; Claus, Théâtre Complet 2, trans Alain Van Crugten.

119. See Esslin, *Artaud*, p. 37, for Artaud's planned staging of *Thyestes*.

Guide to Further Reading

This guide is primarily intended for readers interested in pursuing some of the themes and issues raised in Chapter 3. It is confined to works written in English.

Thyestes: translations

Churchill, Caryl, *Lucius Annaeus Seneca: Thyestes* (London: Nick Hern Books, 1995). A vigorous and basically accurate translation by a major dramatist; written for performance. I say 'basically accurate' because Churchill does not attempt to reproduce Senecan rhetoric.

Elder, Jane, *Lucius Annaeus Seneca: Thyestes. A Tragedy* (Manchester: Cacarnet New Press, 1982). A vigorous and accurate verse translation.

Fitch, John G. (editor), *Seneca: Tragedies* (Cambridge, MA: Harvard University Press, 2002-). Replaces Miller's edition in the Loeb series. At the time of writing the volume containing *Thyestes* is about to appear.

Hadas, Moses, *Seneca's Thyestes* (New York: The Liberal Arts Press, 1957). A serviceable prose translation.

Miller, F.J. (editor), *Seneca: Tragedies* (Cambridge, MA: Harvard University Press, 1917). Old Loeb edition; stodgy, but accurate prose translation accompanying an outdated text.

Share, D., *Seneca in English* (Harmondsworth: Penguin Books, 1998). A stimulating anthology of translated passages from all the tragedies dating from the sixteenth to the twentieth centuries; includes translations and adaptations by Elizabeth I, Shakespeare, Milton, Ted Hughes and many others.

Slavitt, David R., *Seneca: The Tragedies*, vol. 1 (Baltimore: Johns Hopkins University Press, 1992). Not a reliable translation; inserts invented speeches into *Thyestes* as well as references to Claudius, Agrippina, Nero and Seneca himself.

Watling, E.F., *Seneca: Four Tragedies and Octavia* (Harmondsworth: Penguin Books, 1966). Readily available, but unsatisfactory verse translation by an unsympathetic translator.

Thyestes: texts and commentaries

Chaumartin, François-Régis (editor), *Sénèque: Tragédies. Oedipe, Agamemnon, Thyeste*, vol. 2 (Paris: Les Belles Lettres, 1999). Good Latin text, more conservative than Zwierlein's, accompanied by a French translation.

Tarrant, R.J. (editor), *Seneca's Thyestes* (Atlanta, GA: Scholars Press, 1985). Good Latin text accompanied by a valuable commentary.

Zwierlein, O. (editor), *L. Annaei Senecae Tragoediae* (Oxford: Oxford University Press, 1986). The standard text, despite a tendency to unnecessary emendation.

Secondary literature

Boyle, A.J. (editor), *Seneca Tragicus: Ramus Essays on Senecan Drama* (Berwick, Vic.: Aureal Publications, 1983). A landmark collection of essays on all eight tragedies, including two on *Thyestes*.

———— 'Senecan Tragedy: Twelve Propositions', *The Imperial Muse*, vol. 1, *To Juvenal through Ovid* (editor), A.J. Boyle (Berwick, Vic.: Aureal Publications, 1988), pp. 78-101. An important essay which attempts to characterise Senecan tragedy through twelve vigorously defended propositions.

———— *Tragic Seneca: an Essay in the Theatrical Tradition* (London: Routledge, 1997). An examination of all the plays in their social and cultural context; discusses their relationship with Renaissance drama; perhaps the single most important study of Senecan tragedy.

Calder III, William M., 'Seneca: Tragedian of Imperial Rome', *Classical Journal* 72 (1976), pp. 1-11. A lively and sympathetic introduction which acknowledges that 'Atreus is no longer a ridiculous parody. He is a fact with which we live' (p. 2).

———— '*Secreti Loquimur*: an Interpretation of Seneca's *Thyestes*', *Seneca Tragicus: Ramus Essays on Senecan Drama* (Berwick, Vic.: Aureal Publications, 1983), pp. 184-97. An idiosyncratic work, pithily expressed and bristling with ideas.

Davis, P.J., 'The Chorus in Seneca's *Thyestes*', *Classical Quarterly* 39 (1988), pp. 421-35. Examines in detail the thematic and dramatic functions of the four choral odes in *Thyestes*.

———— *Shifting Song: the Chorus in Seneca's Tragedies* (Hildesheim: Olms-Weidmann, 1993). Focusing on the Chorus, this study examines dramatic and thematic issues in the seven complete tragedies.

Harrison, George W.M. (editor), *Seneca in Performance* (London: Classical Press of Wales/Duckworth, 2000). A major collection focusing on the issue of performance. Deals mainly with *Trojan Women*.

Guide to Further Reading

Herington, C.J., 'Senecan Tragedy', *Arion* 5 (1966), pp. 422-71. A major article; the primary inspiration for the twentieth-century revival of interest in Senecan tragedy in the English-speaking world.

Hine, Harry, 'The Structure of Seneca's *Thyestes*', *Papers of the Liverpool Latin Seminar* 3 (1981), pp. 259-75. Concentrates on the thematic function of Act 1.

Meltzer, Gary, 'Dark Wit and Black Humor in Seneca's *Thyestes*', *Transactions of the American Philological Association* 118 (1988), pp. 309-30. Discusses Atreus' use of wit and humour; sees the play as endorsing Stoic positions.

Motto, Anna Lydia and Clark, John R., 'Seneca's *Thyestes* as Melodrama', *Rivista di Studi Classici* 26 (1978), pp. 363-78. Argues that 'Atreus' "victory" ... is no victory whatsoever' (p. 375).

Poe, Joe Park, 'An Analysis of Seneca's *Thyestes*', *Transactions of the American Philological Association* 100 (1969), pp. 355-76. A fine study of Seneca's treatment of the human lust for violence in *Thyestes*.

Schiesaro, Alessandro, 'Forms of Senecan Intertextuality', *Vergilius* 38 (1992), pp. 56-63. Examines the intertextual relationships between Act 1 and *Aeneid* 7.

——— 'Seneca's *Thyestes* and the Morality of Tragic *furor*', *Reflections of Nero: Culture, History, and Representation* (Chapel Hill/London: University of North Carolina Press/Duckworth, 1994), pp. 196-210. Treats Act 1 as staging the play's construction; resists possible political implications.

Segal, C.P., 'Boundary Violation and the Landscape of the Self in Senecan Tragedy', *Interpreting Greek Tragedy: Myth, Poetry, Text* (Ithaca, NY: Cornell University Press, 1986), pp. 315-36. An important study, focusing on *Medea* and *Thyestes*.

Tarrant, R.J., 'Senecan Drama and its Antecedents', *Harvard Studies in Classical Philology* 82 (1978), pp. 213-63. A major study of Seneca's dramatic techniques.

——— 'Greek and Roman in Seneca's Tragedies', *Harvard Studies in Classical Philology* 97 (1995), pp. 215-30. Argues that Senecan tragedy is characterised by fascination with tyrannical power, focus on pathology of the emotions and global background.

155

Bibliography

Texts, translations and commentaries

Ariani, Marco (editor), *Il Teatro italiano, II. La tragedia del Cinquecento* (Torino: Einaudi, 1977).

Ayres, Philip J. (editor), *Ben Jonson: Sejanus His Fall*. (Manchester: Manchester University Press, 1990).

Bate, Jonathan (editor), *William Shakespeare: Titus Andronicus* (London: Routledge, 1995).

Boas, Frederick S. (editor), *The Works of Thomas Kyd* (Oxford: Oxford University Press, 1901).

Bolton, W.F. and Gardner, Jane F. (editors), *Ben Jonson: Catiline* (London: Edward Arnold, 1973).

Boyle, A.J. (editor), *Seneca's Phaedra* (Liverpool: Francis Cairns, 1987).

—— (editor), *Seneca's Troades* (Liverpool: Francis Cairns, 1994).

Chaumartin, François-Régis (editor), *Sénèque: Tragédies. Oedipe, Agamemnon, Thyeste*, vol. 2 (Paris: Les Belles Lettres, 1999).

Claus, Hugo, *Hugo Claus. Thyeste, tragédie d'après Sénèque*, traduite du néerlandais par Maddy Buysse (Paris: Gallimard, 1967).

—— *Théâtre Complet 2: La danse du héron. Thyl Ulenspiegel. Dent pour dent. Thyeste*, translated by Alain Van Crugten (Lausanne: L'Age d'Homme, 1992).

Coffey, M. and Mayer, R. (editors), *Seneca's Phaedra*. Cambridge: Cambridge University Press, 1990.

Daalder, Joost (editor), *Lucius Annaeus Seneca / Jasper Heywood: 'Thyestes' (1560)* (London: Ernest Benn, 1982).

Dunkley, John (editor), *Prosper Jolyot de Crébillon: Electre* (Exeter: University of Exeter, 1980).

Fitch, John G. (editor), *Seneca: Tragedies* (Cambridge, MA: Harvard University Press, 2002-).

Giardina, G.C. (editor), *L. Annaei Senecae Tragoediae* (Bologna: Editrice Compositori Bologna, 1966).

Hine, H.M. (editor), *L. Annaeus Seneca: Medea* (Warminster: Aris & Phillips, 2000).

Hunter, G. K. (editor), *John Marston: Antonio and Mellida: The First Part*. (London: Edward Arnold, 1965).

—— (editor), *John Marston: Antonio's Revenge* (London: Edward Arnold, 1966).

Jocelyn, H.D. (editor), *The Tragedies of Ennius* (Cambridge: Cambridge University Press, 1967).

Lebègue, Raymond (editor), *Robert Garnier: Les Juifves, Bradamante, Poésies Diverses* (Paris: Société les Belles Lettres, 1949).

Lloyd-Jones, Hugh (editor), *Sophocles: Fragments*. Cambridge, MA: Harvard University Press, 1996).

Maidment, James and Logan, William (eds), *The Dramatic Works of John Crowne*, vol. 2 (Edinburgh: William Paterson, 1873).

McIlwraith, A.K. (editor), *Five Elizabethan Tragedies: Thyestes, Gorboduc, The Spanish Tragedy, Arden of Feversham, A Woman Killed with Kindness*. Oxford: Oxford University Press, 1971.

Miller, F.J. (editor), *Seneca, Tragedies*. Cambridge, Mass.: Harvard University Press, 1917.

Moland, Louis (editor), *Oeuvres Complètes de Voltaire*, vol. 7: *Théâtre: Tome Sixième* (Paris: Garnier Frères, 1877).

Mulryne, J.R. (editor), *Thomas Kyd: The Spanish Tragedy* (London: Ernest Benn, 1970).

Nauck, A. (editor), *Tragicorum Graecorum Fragmenta* (Hildesheim: Georg Olms Verlagsbuchhandlung, 1964).

Newton, Thomas (editor), *Seneca His Tenne Tragedies Translated into English. With an Introduction by T.S. Eliot* (London: Constable and Co. Ltd, 1927 [1581]).

Ribbeck, Otto (editor), *Tragicorum Romanorum Fragmenta* (Hildesheim: Georg Olms Verlagsbuchhandlung, 1962).

Rutenberg, Michael Elliot (editor), *Oedipus of Lucius Annaeus Seneca* (Wauconda, Illinois: Bolchazy-Carducci Publishers, Inc., 1999).

Seneca, *Seneca's Thyestes*, translated by Moses Hadas (New York: The Liberal Arts Press, 1957).

—— *Four Tragedies and Octavia*, translated by E.F. Watling (Harmondsworth: Penguin Books, 1966).

—— *Lucius Annaeus Seneca: Thyestes. A Tragedy*, translated by Jane Elder (Manchester: Cacarnet New Press, 1982).

—— *Seneca: The Tragedies*, vol. 1, translated by David R. Slavitt (Baltimore: Johns Hopkins University Press, 1992).

—— *Lucius Annaeus Seneca: Thyestes*, translated by Caryl Churchill (London: Nick Hern Books, 1995).

Share, D., *Seneca in English* (Harmondsworth: Penguin Books, 1998).

Smith, Emma (editor), *Thomas Kyd: The Spanish Tragedie* (Harmondsworth: Penguin Books, 1998).

Sturgess, Keith (editor), *John Marston: The Malcontent and Other Plays* (Oxford: Oxford University Press, 1997).

Tarrant, R.J. (editor), *Seneca: Agamemnon* (Cambridge: Cambridge University Press, 1976).

Bibliography

—— (editor), *Seneca's Thyestes* (Atlanta, GA.: Scholars Press, 1985).

Vitu, Auguste (editor), *J. De Crébillon: Théâtre Complet* (Paris: Libraire Garnier Frères, 1923).

Waith, Eugene M. (editor), *Shakespeare: Titus Andronicus* (Oxford: Oxford University Press, 1984).

Warmington, E.H. (editor), *Remains of Old Latin 1: Ennius and Caecilius* (Cambridge, MA: Harvard University Press, 1956).

—— (editor), *Remains of Old Latin 2: Livius Andronicus, Naevius, Pacuvius and Accius* (Cambridge, MA: Harvard University Press, 1957).

Wilson, John Harold (editor), *John Crowne: City Politiques* (London: Edward Arnold, 1967).

Wright, J.W., *Thyestes: A Tragedy, translated out of Seneca: to which is added Mock-Thyestes, in Burlesque* (London: T.R. and N.T. for Allen Banks, 1674).

Zwierlein, O. (editor), *L. Annaei Senecae Tragoediae* (Oxford: Oxford University Press, 1986).

Secondary literature

Ahl, Frederick, 'Seneca and Chaucer: Translating both Poetry and Sense', in *Seneca in Performance* (London: Classical Press of Wales/Duckworth, 2000), pp. 151-71.

Amoroso, Filippo, 'Messa in scena di Seneca tragico', in *Atti del XIV Congresso Internazionale di Studi sul Dramma Antico* (Syracuse: Istituto Nazionale del Dramma Antico, 1993), pp. 87-100.

—— 'Spettacoli Senecani nel Ventesimo Secolo: l'attività dell'Istituto Nazionale del Dramma Antico', in *Atti dei convegni 'Il mondo scenico di Plauto' e 'Seneca e i volti del potere'* (Genova: Dipartimento di Archeologia, Fililogia Classica e loro Tradizioni, 1995), pp. 219-24.

Armato, Rosario P., 'The Play is the Thing: a Study of Giraldi's Orbecche and Its Senecan Antecedents', in *Medieval Epic to the 'Epic Theater' of Brecht*, edited by Rosario P. Armato and John M. Spalek (Los Angeles: University of Southern California Press, 1968), pp. 57-83.

Aslan, Odette, *Roger Blin and Twentieth Century Playwrights* (Cambridge: Cambridge University Press, 1988).

Audino, Antonio, 'Seneca e Plauto fra i dialetti', *Il Sole 24 Ore* (22 March 1998), p. 36.

Ayres, Philip J., 'The Nature of Jonson's Roman History', *English Literary Renaissance* 16 (1986), pp. 166-81.

Babula, William, 'The Avenger and the Satirist: John Marston's Malevole', in *The Elizabethan Theatre VI*, edited by G.R. Hibbard (Ontario: Macmillan Company of Canada Limited, 1975), pp. 48-58.

159

Bacquet, Paul, 'L'Imitation de Sénèque dans "Gorboduc" de Sackville et Norton', in *Les Tragédies de Sénèque et le Théâtre de la Renaissance* (Paris: Editions du Centre National de la Recherche Scientifique, 1964), pp. 153-74.

Baines, Barbara, 'Antonio's Revenge: Marston's Play on Revenge Plays', *Studies in English Literature, 1500-1900* 23 (1983), pp. 277-94.

Baker, Howard, *Induction to Tragedy: a Study in a Development of Form in Gorboduc, The Spanish Tragedy, and Titus Andronicus* (New York: Russell and Russell, 1939).

Barone, C., 'Gassman, Squarzina e il Tieste di Seneca', *Dioniso* 2 (1980), pp. 246-56.

Barton, Anne, *Ben Jonson, Dramatist* (Cambridge: Cambridge University Press, 1984).

Bate, Jonathan, *Shakespeare and Ovid* (Oxford: Oxford University Press, 1993).

Berland, Ellen, 'The Function of Irony in Marston's *Antonio and Mellida*', *Studies in Philology* 66 (1969), pp. 739-55.

Blin, Roger, *Souvenirs et Propos* (Paris: Gallimard, 1986).

Boas, F.S., *University Drama in the Tudor Age* (Oxford: Oxford University Press, 1914).

Bowers, Fredson Thayer, *Elizabethan Revenge Tragedy, 1587-1642* (Gloucester, MA: P. Smith, 1940/1959).

Boyle, A.J., '*Hic epulis locus*: the Tragic Worlds of Seneca's *Agamemnon* and *Thyestes*', in *Seneca Tragicus: Ramus Essays on Senecan Drama* (Berwick, Vic.: Aureal Publications, 1983), pp. 199-228.

——— (editor), *Seneca Tragicus: Ramus Essays on Senecan Drama* (Berwick, Vic.: Aureal Publications, 1983).

——— 'Senecan Tragedy: Twelve Propositions', in *The Imperial Muse*, vol. 1: *To Juvenal through Ovid* (Berwick, Vic.: Aureal Publications, 1988), pp. 78-101.

——— *Tragic Seneca: an Essay in the Theatrical Tradition* (London: Routledge, 1997).

Braden, G., 'The Rhetoric and Psychology of Power in the Dramas of Seneca', *Arion* 9 (1970), pp. 5-41.

——— *Renaissance Tragedy and the Senecan Tradition: Anger's Privilege* (New Haven, Conn.: Yale University Press, 1985).

Braun, L., 'La forza del visibile nelle tragedie di Seneca', *Dioniso* 52 (1981), pp. 36-9, 109-24.

——— 'Sind Senecas Tragödien Bühnenstucke oder Rezitationsdramen?', *Res Publica Litterarum: Studies in the Classical Tradition* 5 (1982), pp. 43-52.

Braunmuller, A.R. and Hattaway, Michael (editors), *Cambridge Companion to English Renaissance Drama* (Cambridge: Cambridge University Press, 1990).

Bibliography

Brook, Peter, 'Peter Brook Talking to Frank Cox about Seneca's *Oedipus*', *Plays and Players* 17 no. 7 (1968), pp. 50-1.

Bruce, George, 'Glasgow: Seneca's *Thyestes*', *Sunday Times* (16 November 1975), p. 36a.

Calder III, William M., 'Seneca: Tragedian of Imperial Rome', *Classical Journal* 72 (1976), pp. 1-11.

——— '*Secreti Loquimur*: an Interpretation of Seneca's *Thyestes*', in *Seneca Tragicus: Ramus Essays on Senecan Drama*, edited by A.J. Boyle (Berwick, Vic.: Aureal Publications, 1983), pp. 184-97.

——— 'Seneca *Thyestes* 101-106', *Classical Philology* 79 (1984), pp. 225f.

Caputi, Anthony, *John Marston, Satirist* (New York: Cornell University Press, 1961).

Carbone, Martin E., 'The *Octavia*: Structure, Date and Authenticity', *Phoenix* 31 (1977), pp. 48-67.

Charlton, H.B., *The Senecan Tradition in Renaissance Tragedy: a Reissue of an Essay Published in 1921* (Manchester: Manchester University Press, 1946).

Coffey, Michael, 'Notes on the History of Augustan and Early Imperial Tragedy', in *Studies in Honour of T.B.L. Webster*, edited by J.H. Betts, J.T. Hooker and J.R. Green (Bristol: Bristol Classical Press, 1986), pp. 46-52.

Cournot, Michel, 'Un Sénèque un peu anachronique et qui vous étourdit de beauté', *Le Monde* (7 December 1999), Culture.

Coveney, Michael, 'Seneca's *Thyestes*', *Observer* (12 June 1994), R9.

Cunliffe, John W., *The Influence of Seneca on Elizabethan Tragedy* (New York: Gordon Press, 1893/1974).

D'Amico, Masolino, 'Tieste ovvero la vendetta mafiosa', *La Stampa* (22 March 1998), Spettacoli 28.

Daalder, Joost, 'The Role of "Senex" in Kyd's *The Spanish Tragedy*', *Comparative Drama* 20 (1986), pp. 247-60.

Davis, P.J., '*Vindicat omnes natura sibi:* a Reading of Seneca's *Phaedra*', in *Seneca Tragicus: Ramus Essays on Senecan Drama*, edited by A.J Boyle (Berwick, Vic.: Aureal Publications, 1983), pp. 114-27.

——— 'Structure and Meaning in the *Eclogues* of Calpurnius Siculus', *Ramus* 16 (1987), pp. 32-54.

——— 'The Chorus in Seneca's *Thyestes*', *Classical Quarterly* 39 (1988), pp. 421-35.

——— *Shifting Song: the Chorus in Seneca's Tragedies* (Hildesheim: Olms-Weidmann, 1993).

——— 'Rewriting Seneca: Garnier's *Hippolyte*', *Classical and Modern Literature* 17 (1997), pp. 293-318.

de Armas, Frederick A., 'Astraea's Fall: Senecan Images in Shakespeare's *Titus Andronicus* and Calderon's *La vida es sueno*', in *Parallel Lives: Spanish and English National Drama 1580-1680*, edited by Louise and Peter Fothergill-Payne (Lewisburg: Bucknell University Press, 1991), pp. 302-21.

DiMauro, Damon, 'Garnier's Historical Sources in *Les Juifves*', *Renaissance and Reformation / Renaissance et Reforme* 17 (1993), pp. 21-31.

Dupont, Florence, *L'Acteur-roi, ou le théâtre dans la Rome antique* (Paris: Les Belles Lettres, 1985).

―――― *Les monstres de Sénèque* (Paris: Éditions Belin, 1995).

Eliot, T.S., 'Seneca in Elizabethan Translation', in *Selected Essays* (London: Faber & Faber, 1951), pp. 65-105.

Esslin, Martin, *Artaud* (London: John Calder, 1976).

Fantham, Elaine, 'Production of Seneca's *Trojan Women*, Ancient? and Modern', in *Seneca in Performance*, edited by George W.M. Harrison (London: Classical Press of Wales/Duckworth, 2000), pp. 13-26.

Feeney, D.C., *The Gods in Epic: Poets and Critics of the Classical Tradition* (Oxford: Oxford University Press, 1991).

Finkelpearl, Philip J., *John Marston of the Middle Temple: an Elizabethan Dramatist in his Social Setting* (Cambridge, MA: Harvard University Press, 1969).

Fitch, John G., 'Sense-Pauses and Relative Dating in Seneca, Sophocles and Shakespeare', *American Journal of Philology* 102 (1981), pp. 289-307.

―――― 'Playing Seneca?', in *Seneca in Performance*, edited by George W.M. Harrison (London: Classical Press of Wales/Duckworth, 2000), pp. 1-12.

Fraser, Antonia, *King Charles II* (London: Weidenfeld & Nicolson, 1979).

Gassman, Vittorio, *Tieste di Seneca* (Bologna: Licinio Cappelli Editore, 1953).

Gigon, Olof, 'Bemerkungen zu Senecas *Thyestes*', *Philologus* 93 (1938/39), pp. 176-83.

Goldberg, Sander M., 'Going for Baroque: Seneca and the English', in *Seneca in Performance* (London: Classical Press of Wales/Duckworth, 2000), pp. 209-31.

Gratwick, A.S., 'Drama', in *Cambridge History of Classical Literature*, vol. 2: *Latin Literature*, edited by E.J. Kenney and W.V. Clausen (Cambridge: Cambridge University Press, 1982), pp. 77-137.

Griffin, Miriam T., *Seneca: a Philosopher in Politics* (Oxford: Oxford University Press, 1976).

―――― *Nero: the End of a Dynasty* (London: Batsford, 1984).

Gross, John, 'A Full-bodied, Bloody Wine', *Sunday Telegraph* (12 June 1994), p. 7.

Bibliography

Hall, Edith, 'Things Go Badly', *Times Literary Supplement* (1 July 1994), p. 18.

Halliwell, James O., *A Dictionary of Old English Plays existing either in print or in manuscript from the earliest times to the close of the seventeenth century* (London: John Russell Smith, 1860).

Hamilton, A.C., *The Early Shakespeare* (San Marino, CA: The Huntington Library, 1967).

Hansen, Jørgen Wildt, 'Two Notes on Seneca and *Titus Andronicus*', *Anglia* 93 (1975), pp. 161-5.

Harrison, George W.M., '*Semper ego auditor tantum*? Performance and Physical Setting of Seneca's Plays', in *Seneca in Performance*, edited by George W.M. Harrison (London: Classical Press of Wales/Duckworth, 2000), pp. 137-49.

—— (editor), *Seneca in Performance* (London: Classical Press of Wales/Duckworth, 2000).

Henderson, John, 'Statius' *Thebaid*/Form Premade', *Proceedings of the Cambridge Philological Society* 37 (1991), pp. 30-79.

Herington, C.J., 'Senecan Tragedy', *Arion* 5 (1966), pp. 422-71.

—— 'The Younger Seneca', in *Cambridge History of Classical Literature*, vol. 2: *Latin Literature*, edited by E.J. Kenney and W.V. Clausen (Cambridge: Cambridge University Press, 1982), pp. 511-30.

Herrick, Marvin T., 'Senecan Influence in *Gorboduc*', in *Studies in Speech and Drama in Honor of Alexander M. Drummond* (Ithaca, NY: Cornell University Press, 1944), pp. 78-104.

Hill, Eugene D., 'Senecan and Vergilian Perspectives in *The Spanish Tragedy*', *English Literary Renaissance* 15 (1985), pp. 143-65.

Hine, Harry, 'The Structure of Seneca's *Thyestes*', *Papers of the Liverpool Latin Seminar* 3 (1981), pp. 259-75.

Hollingsworth, Anthony, 'Recitational Poetry and Senecan Tragedy: Is There a Similarity?', *Classical World* 94 (2001), pp. 135-44.

Horne, P.R., *The Tragedies of Giambattista Cinthio Giraldi* (Oxford: Oxford University Press, 1962).

Hunter, G.K., 'Seneca and English Tragedy', in *Seneca*, edited by C.D.N. Costa (London: Routledge & Kegan Paul, 1974), pp. 166-204.

—— 'Ironies of Justice in *The Spanish Tragedy*', *Renaissance Drama* 8 (1965), pp. 89-104.

—— 'Seneca and the Elizabethans: a Case-Study in "Influence" ', *Shakespeare Survey* 20 (1967), pp. 17-26.

—— 'Shakespeare and the Traditions of Tragedy', in *Cambridge Companion to Shakespeare Studies*, edited by Stanley Wells (Cambridge: Cambridge University Press, 1986), pp. 123-41.

Hutchinson, G.O., *Latin Literature from Seneca to Juvenal: a Critical Study* (Oxford: Oxford University Press, 1993).

James, Heather, *Shakespeare's Troy: Drama, Politics and the*

Translation of Empire (Cambridge: Cambridge University Press, 1997).

Keen, Antony G., 'Review: Lucius Annaeus Seneca's *Thyestes*', *Didaskalia* 1 (August 1994), didaskalia.berkeley.edu.

Kenney, E.J. and Clausen, W.V. (editors), *Cambridge History of Classical Literature*, vol. 2: *Latin Literature* (Cambridge: Cambridge University Press, 1982).

Kermode, Frank, *Shakespeare's Language* (London: Allen Lane, The Penguin Press, 2000).

Kiefer, Frederick, 'Seneca's Influence on Elizabethan Tragedy: an Annotated Bibliography', *Research Opportunities in Renaissance Drama* 21 (1978), pp. 17-34.

———— 'Senecan Influence: a Bibliographic Supplement', *Research Opportunities in Renaissance Drama* 28 (1985), pp. 129-42.

Kragelund, P., 'Senecan Tragedy: Back on Stage', *Classica et Mediaevalia* 50 (1999), pp. 235-47.

La Penna, Antonio, 'Atreo e Tieste sulle scene Romane', in *Studi Classici in Onore di Quintino Cataudella* (Catania: Università di Catania, 1972), pp. 357-71.

Lancaster, Henry Carrington, *A History of French Dramatic Literature in the Seventeenth Century. Part II: The Period of Corneille 1635-1651* (Baltimore: Johns Hopkins University Press, 1932).

Law, Robert Adger, 'The Roman Background of *Titus Andronicus*', *Studies in Philology* 40 (1943), pp. 145-53.

Lebek, W.D., 'Seneca's Agamemnon in Pompeji (*CIL* iv 6698)', *Zeitschrift für Papyrologie und Epigraphik* 59 (1985), pp. 1-6.

Lefèvre, E., *Der Einfluss Senecas auf das europäische Drama* (Darmstadt: Wissenschaftliche Buchgesellschaft, 1978).

———— 'Die philosophische Bedeutung der Seneca-Tragödie am Beispiel des Thyestes', in *Aufstieg und Niedergang der römischen Welt* (Berlin: Walter de Gruyter, 1985), pp. 1263-83.

Lucas, F.L., *Seneca and Elizabethan Tragedy* (Cambridge: Cambridge University Press, 1922).

Macdonald, William L., *The Architecture of the Roman Empire: an Introductory Study* (New Haven: Yale University Press, 1982).

Mader, Gottfried, 'Paradox and Perspective. Two Examples from Seneca's Tragedies (*Thy.* 470; *Ag.* 869)', *Acta Classica* 25 (1982), pp. 71-83.

———— '*Quod nolunt velint*: Deference and Doublespeak at Seneca, *Thyestes* 334-335', *Classical Journal* 94 (1998), pp. 31-47.

Marchesi, Concetto, 'La prima rappresentazione del Tieste di Seneca', *Rinascita* X.1 (1953), pp. 45-7.

Marshall, C.W., 'Location! Location! Location! Choral Absence and Dramatic Space in Seneca's *Troades*', in *Seneca in Performance*, edited by George W.M. Harrison (London: Classical Press of Wales/Duckworth, 2000), pp. 27-51.

Bibliography

Mayer, Roland, *Seneca: Phaedra* (London: Duckworth, 2002).

Mayrhofer, Colin, 'The Complete Plays of Seneca', *Didaskalia* 3 (Spring/Summer 1996), didaskalia.berkeley.edu.

Meltzer, Gary, 'Dark Wit and Black Humor in Seneca's *Thyestes*', *Transactions of the American Philological Association* 118 (1988), pp. 309-30.

Mercer, Peter, *'Hamlet' and the Acting of Revenge* (Iowa City: University of Iowa Press, 1987).

Miola, Robert S., *'Titus Andronicus* and the Mythos of Shakespeare's Rome', *Shakespeare Studies* 14 (1981), pp. 85-98.

―――― *Shakespeare and Classical Tragedy: the Influence of Seneca* (Oxford: Oxford University Press, 1992).

Monteleone, Ciro, 'I modelli di Seneca nel prologo del *Thyestes*', *Giornale Italiano di Filologia* 32 (1980), p. 2.

―――― *Il 'Thyestes' di Seneca: sentieri ermeneutici* (Fasano: Schena Editore, 1991).

Morrison, Mary, *The Tragedies of G.-B. Giraldi Cinthio: the Transformation of Narrative into Stage Play* (Lewiston, New York: Edwin Mellen Press, 1997).

Motto, Anna Lydia and Clark, John R., 'Senecan Tragedy: a Critique of Scholarly Trends', *Renaissance Drama* 6 (1973), pp. 219-35.

―――― 'Seneca's *Thyestes* as Melodrama', *Rivista di Studi Classici* 26 (1978), pp. 363-78.

―――― *Senecan Tragedy* (Amsterdam: Adolf M. Hakkert, 1988).

Mueller, Martin, *Children of Oedipus, and other essays on the imitation of Greek tragedy, 1550-1800* (Toronto: University of Toronto Press, 1980).

Murray, Oswyn, 'Verbal Play', *Times Literary Supplement* (2-8 September 1988), p. 964.

Nelson, Alan H., *Records of Early English Drama. Cambridge* (Toronto: Toronto University Press, 1989).

Nisbet, R.G.M., 'The Dating of Seneca's Tragedies, with Special Reference to *Thyestes*', *Papers of the Leeds International Latin Seminar* 6 (1990), pp. 95-114.

Pandolfi, Vito, 'Tieste dopo duemila anni', *Dramma* (1953), pp. 44-7.

Paratore, Ettore, 'Seneca autore di teatro', in *Seneca e il Teatro: Atti dell' VIII Congresso internazionale di Studi sul Dramma Antico. Siracusa, 9-12 Settembre 1981*, edited by Filippo Amoroso (Siracusa: Istituto Nazionale del Dramma Antico, 1981), pp. 29-46.

―――― 'Il prologo del Agamemnon e quello del Thyestes di Seneca', *Vichiana* 11 (1982), pp. 226-34.

Picone, G., 'Il significato politico di alcuni anacronismi nel Thyestes di Seneca', *Pan* 3 (1976), pp. 61-7.

―――― *La Fabula e il Regno. Studi sul Thyestes di Seneca* (Palermo: Palumbo, 1984).

Poe, Joe Park, 'An Analysis of Seneca's *Thyestes*', *Transactions of the American Philological Association* 100 (1969), pp. 355-76.

Pratt, N.T., *Seneca's Drama* (Chapel Hill: University of North Carolina Press, 1983).

Raboni, Giovanni, 'Un "Tieste" di solo donne che pare uscito da uno spot', *Corriere della Sera* (7 April 1991), p. 20.

Raby, Gyllian, 'Seneca's *Trojan Women*: Identity and Survival in the Aftermath of War', in *Seneca in Performance*, edited by George W.M. Harrison (London: Classical Press of Wales/Duckworth, 2000), pp. 173-95.

Ratliff, John D., 'Hieronimo Explains Himself', *Studies in Philology* 54 (1957), pp. 112-18.

Regenbogen, O., 'Schmerz und Tod in den Tragödien Senecas', *Vorträge der Bibliothek Warburg* 7 (1927/28), pp. 167-218.

Reynolds, L.D., *Texts and Transmission: a Survey of the Latin Classics* (Oxford: Oxford University Press, 1983).

Rosenmeyer, Thomas G., 'Seneca's *Oedipus* and Performance: the Manto Scene', in *Theater and Society in the Classical World*, edited by R. Scodel (Ann Arbor: University of Michigan Press, 1993), pp. 235-44.

Rossi, Elena, *Una metafora presa alla lettera: Le membra lacerate della famiglia. Tieste di Seneca e i rifaciamenti moderni* (Pisa: ETS, 1989).

Salino, Brigitte, 'Les monstres de Sénèque ne font pas de quartier', *Le Monde* (21 October 1995), Culture.

Schiesaro, Alessandro, 'Forms of Senecan Intertextuality', *Vergilius* 38 (1992), pp. 56-63.

———— 'Seneca's *Thyestes* and the Morality of Tragic *furor*', in *Reflections of Nero: Culture, History and Representation* (Chapel Hill/London: University of North Carolina Press/Duckworth, 1994), pp. 196-210.

Schmitt, Olivier, 'Thyeste à Nanterre-Amandiers. Le crime des crimes', *Le Monde* (8 October 1995), Culture.

Schubert, Christoph, *Studien zum Nerobild in der lateinischen Dichtung der Antike* (Stuttgart & Leipzig: B.G. Teubner, 1998).

Segal, C.P., 'Boundary Violation and the Landscape of the Self in Senecan Tragedy', in *Interpreting Greek Tragedy: Myth, Poetry, Text* (Ithaca, NY: Cornell University Press, 1986), pp. 315-36.

Segala, Elisabetta and Sciortino, Ida, *Domus Aurea* (Milan: Electa, 1999).

Seidensticker, B., *Die Gesprächsverdichtung in den Tragödien Senecas* (Heidelberg: Carl Winter, 1969).

———— 'Maius solito. Senecas *Thyestes* und die tragoedia rhetorica', *Antike und Abendland* 31 (1985), pp. 116-36.

Seidensticker, Bernd and Armstrong, David, 'Seneca Tragicus 1878-

Bibliography

1978 (with Addenda 1979ff.)', *Aufstieg und Niedergang der römischen Welt* II.32.2 (1985), pp. 916-68.

Seidmann, David, 'Les Sources des Juifves de R. Garnier', *Bibliotheque d'Humanisme et Renaissance* 28 (1966), pp. 75-7.

Shelton, Jo-Ann, 'Problems of Time in Seneca's *Hercules Furens* and *Thyestes*', *California Studies in Classical Antiquity* 8 (1975), pp. 257-69.

Small, Christopher, 'Atrocity in a Fog', *Glasgow Herald* (Friday 7 November 1975), p. 5.

Smith, Bruce R., *Ancient Scripts and Modern Experience on the English Stage: 1500-1700* (Princeton: Princeton University Press, 1988).

Smith, John Hazel, 'Seneca's Tragedies: a Tentative Checklist of Fifteenth-, Sixteenth-, and Seventeenth-Century Printings', *Research Opportunities in Renaissance Drama* 10 (1967), pp. 49-74.

Steidle, Wolf, 'Die Gestalt des Thyest', in *Senecas Tragödien*, edited by E. Lefèvre (Darmstadt: Wissenschaftliche Buchgesellschaft, 1972), pp. 490-9.

Stroh, W., ' "Give us your applause!": the World of Theatre', in *Gladiators and Caesars: the Power of Spectacle in Ancient Rome*, edited by Eckart Köhne and Cornelia Ewigleben (London: British Museum Press, 2000), pp. 103-24.

Stroh, Wilfried and Breitenberger, Barbara., 'Inszenierung Senecas', in *Orchestra: Drama Mythos Bühne, Festschrift für Hellmut Flashar*, edited by Anton Bierl and Peter von Möllendorf (Stuttgart: Teubner, 1994), pp. 248-69.

Sutherland, Jean Murray, 'Shakespeare and Seneca: a Symbolic Language for Tragedy' (Ann Arbor, MI: Dissertation Abstracts International, 1986).

Sutton, D.F., *Seneca on the Stage* (Leiden: E.J. Brill, 1986).

Taplin, O., 'Did Greek Dramatists Write Stage Instructions?', *Proceedings of the Cambridge Philological Society* 203 (23) (1977a), pp. 121-32.

―――― *The Stagecraft of Aeschylus: the Dramatic Use of Exits and Entrances in Greek Tragedy* (Oxford: Oxford University Press, 1977b).

Tarrant, R J., 'Senecan Drama and its Antecedents', *Harvard Studies in Classical Philology* 82 (1978), pp. 213-63.

―――― 'Greek and Roman in Seneca's Tragedies', *Harvard Studies in Classical Philology* 97 (1995), pp. 215-30.

Taylor, Paul, 'Viler than Violence', *Independent* (8 June 1994), p. 25.

Thornber, Robin, '*Thyestes*, Manchester', *Guardian* (7 June 1994), T6.

Tobin, Ronald W., 'Nourriture, bienséances et tragédie: l'exemple de Thyeste', *Littératures Classiques* 16 (1992), pp. 169-80.

Van Tieghem, P., *La Littérature latine de la Renaissance* (Geneva: Slatkine Reprints, 1966).

Vessey, David, *Statius and the Thebaid* (Cambridge: Cambridge University Press, 1973).

Volk, Katharina, 'Putting Andromacha on Stage: a Performer's Perspective', in *Seneca in Performance*, edited by George W.M. Harrison (London: Classical Press of Wales/Duckworth, 2000), pp. 197-208.

Walker, B., 'Review of Zwierlein, Die Rezitationsdramen Senecas', *Classical Philology* 64 (1969), pp. 183-7.

Wardle, Irving, 'The Greeks Had Words For It, We Don't', *Independent* (12 June 1994), p. 25.

Watson, Robert N., 'Tragedy', in *Cambridge Companion to English Renaissance Drama*, edited by A.R. Braunmuller and Michael Hattaway (Cambridge: Cambridge University Press, 1990), pp. 301-51.

White, Arthur F., *John Crowne: His Life and Dramatic Works* (Cleveland: Western Reserve University Press, 1922).

Zwierlein, Otto, *Die Rezitationsdramen Senecas* (Meisenheim-am-Glan: Verlag Anton Hain, 1966).

Chronology

BC
4-1: Birth of Lucius Annaeus Seneca in Corduba, southern Spain

AD
14-37: Rule of Tiberius
37-41: Rule of Gaius Caligula
41-54: Rule of Claudius
41:   Seneca banished to Corsica for alleged adultery with Julia Livilla
49:   Seneca recalled from exile and appointed tutor to the young Nero
54-68: Rule of Nero
55:   Nero murders Britannicus
55/56: Composition of *On Mercy*
59:   Nero murders Agrippina
62:   Death of Burrus; Nero murders Octavia; Seneca withdraws from public life: composition of *Thyestes*?
64:   Great fire of Rome; Nero on stage in Naples
65:   Seneca's forced suicide for alleged involvement in Piso's conspiracy
66-7: Nero in Greece
68:   Revolt of Vindex; Nero's death
91:   Publication of Statius' *Thebaid*
1484: Publication of the first printed edition of Seneca's tragedies in Ferrara
1541: Cinzio's *Orbecche*
1560: Publication of Heywood's first English translation of *Thyestes*
1562: Norton and Sackville's *Gorboduc*
1583: Garnier's *Les Juifves*
1587: Kyd's *The Spanish Tragedy*
1591: Shakespeare's *Titus Andronicus*
1599: Marston's *Antonio and Mellida*
1600: Marston's *Antonio's Revenge*
1603: Jonson's *Sejanus*
1611: Jonson's *Catiline*
1661: Gronovius' edition of Seneca's tragedies, the first to be based on both manuscript traditions (A and E)

1674: Wright's *Thyestes* and *Mock-Thyestes*
1681: Crowne's *Thyestes*
1707: Crébillon's *Atrée et Thyeste*
1770: Voltaire's *Les Pélopides*
1953: Production of *Thyestes* in Rome
1966: Claus' *Thyestes*
1975: Production of *Thyestes* in Glasgow
1987: Production of *Thyestes* at Harvard University
1991: Productions of *Thyestes* in Milan and Segesta
1994: Production of *Thyestes* in Manchester and London
1994: Production of *Thyestes* in Paris
1995: Production of *Thyestes* in Paris
1998: Production of *Thyestes* in Rome
1999: Production of *Thyestes* in Paris

Index